CULTURAL STUDIES
AND THE STUDY OF
POPULAR CULTURE

for Xiang

CULTURAL STUDIES AND THE STUDY OF POPULAR CULTURE

Third edition

John Storey

Edinburgh University Press

© John Storey, 1996, 2003, 2010

First edition published in 1996 by Edinburgh University Press.

Edinburgh University Press Ltd
22 George Square, Edinburgh

Reprinted 2011

www.euppublishing.com

Typeset in Sabon by Hewer Text UK Ltd, Edinburgh
Printed and bound in Great Britain by CPI Antony
Rowe, Chippenham and Eastbourne

A CIP record for this book is available from the British Library

ISBN 978 0 7486 4051 5 (hardback)
ISBN 978 0 7486 4038 6 (paperback)

The right of John Storey
to be identified as author of this work
has been asserted in accordance with
the Copyright, Designs and Patents Act 1988.

CONTENTS

PREFACE TO THIRD EDITION

Cultural Studies and the Study of Popular Culture, third edition, is a revised, rewritten and expanded version of the second edition.

I would like to take this opportunity to thank all those who have contributed, knowingly and unknowingly, to the writing of this book, especially family, friends, colleagues, and students (past and present). I would particularly like to thank my daughter Jenny Storey for her help and support throughout. Finally, I would like to thank Zhou Xiangyan for taking me to Wai Ling Ding.

Guangzhou and Sunderland 2009

1

CULTURAL STUDIES AND THE STUDY OF POPULAR CULTURE: AN INTRODUCTION

The aim of this book is twofold: first, to introduce students and other interested readers to the study of contemporary popular culture; and second, to suggest a map of the development of British cultural studies through a discussion of a range of theories and methods for the study of popular culture. I have not attempted an elaborate mapping of the field. Rather, my aim has been to bring together under discussion a range of approaches which have made a significant contribution to the development of the cultural studies approach to the study of contemporary popular culture. It is hoped the book will provide a useful introduction – and range of *usable* theories and methods – for students new to the field, and a critical overview for those more familiar with the procedures and politics of cultural studies.[1]

CULTURAL STUDIES AND POPULAR CULTURE

Cultural studies is not a monolithic body of theories and methods. Stuart Hall (1992) makes this very clear:

> Cultural Studies has multiple discourses; it has a number of different histories. It is a whole set of formations; it has its own different conjunctures and moments in the past. It included

1

many different kinds of work ... It always was a set of unstable formations ... It had many trajectories; many people had and have different theoretical positions, all of them in contention. (278)

Cultural studies has always been an unfolding discourse, responding to changing historical and political conditions and always marked by debate, disagreement and intervention. For example, in the late 1970s the centrality of class in cultural studies was disrupted first by feminism's insistence on the importance of gender, and then by black students raising questions about the invisibility of 'race' in much cultural studies analysis. It is simply not possible *now* to think of cultural studies and popular culture, for example, without also thinking about the enormous contribution to the study of popular culture made by feminism. In the early 1970s, such a connection would have been far from obvious.

Although it is possible to point to degree programmes, to journals, to conferences and to academic associations, there is no simple answer to the question, *what is British cultural studies?* The problem is that so much of British cultural studies is not in origin British; it comes from, for example, France (Louis Althusser, Roland Barthes, Pierre Bourdieu, Michel de Certeau, Michel Foucault, Jacques Lacan), Austria (Sigmund Freud), Germany (Karl Marx), Italy (Antonio Gramsci), Russia (Mikhail Bakhtin, Valentin Volosinov), Switzerland (Ferdinand de Saussure). Therefore, although British cultural studies tends to be associated with the work of Richard Hoggart, Raymond Williams, E. P. Thompson, and Stuart Hall,[2] the various 'appropriations' of work from outside the UK make this position not as straightforward as it might at first appear.

Cultural studies works with an inclusive definition of culture. That is, it is a 'democratic' project in the sense that rather than study only what Matthew Arnold called 'the best which has been thought and said' (Arnold 2009, F. R. Leavis 2009), cultural studies is committed to examining *all* that has been thought and said (although in practice, as I will shortly discuss, most effort has been focused on popular culture). To put it simply, culture is how we live nature (including our own biology); it is the shared meanings we

2

make and encounter in our everyday lives. Culture is not something essential, embodied in particular 'texts' (that is, any commodity, object or event that can be made to signify), it is the practices and processes of making meanings with and from the 'texts' we encounter in our everyday lives.[3] In this way, then, cultures are made from the production, circulation and consumption of meanings. To share a culture, therefore, is to interpret the world – make it meaningful – in recognisably similar ways.

To see culture as the practices and processes of making shared meanings does not mean that cultural studies believes that cultures are harmonious, organic wholes. On the contrary, cultural studies maintains that the 'texts' from which cultures are made are 'multi-accentual' (Volosinov 1973). That is, they can be made to mean in many different ways. Given this, conflict over making the world mean – insisting on the 'right' meaning(s) – is almost inevitable. It is this conflict – the relations between culture and power – which is the core interest of cultural studies. How cultural studies thinks of the relations between culture and power is informed most often by the work of Antonio Gramsci and Michel Foucault. As Stuart Hall observed in one of the foundational essays of British cultural studies, 'Foucault and Gramsci between them account for much of the most productive work on concrete analysis now being undertaken in the field' (Hall 1996a). Although Hall wrote this in 1980, and between then and now cultural studies has been influenced by (and has in turn influenced) feminism, post-structuralism, post-colonial theory, psychoanalysis, postmodernism, and queer theory, I would argue that the work of Gramsci and Foucault is still fundamental to cultural studies as it is practised in the UK.

The introduction of Gramsci's concept of 'hegemony' (Gramsci 1971) into British cultural studies in the early 1970s brought about a rethinking of popular culture (Storey 2009a, 2010). It did this in two ways. First of all it produced a rethinking of the politics of popular culture; popular culture was now seen as a key site for the production and reproduction of hegemony. Capitalist industrial societies are societies divided unequally in terms of, for example, ethnicity, gender, generation, sexuality and social class. Cultural studies argues that popular culture is one of the principal sites

3

where these divisions are established and contested; that is, popular culture is an arena of struggle and negotiation between the interests of dominant groups and the interests of subordinate groups. Working within the framework of hegemony, Hall deploys the concept of 'articulation' (Hall 1982, 1996b) to explain the processes of ideological struggle.[4] Hall's use plays on the term's double meaning to express and connect: first, it is an 'articulation' in that meaning has to be expressed (the 'text' has to be made to signify); second, it is an 'articulation' in that meaning is always expressed in a specific context (connected to another context and the 'text' could be made to signify something quite different). A 'text', therefore, is not the issuing source of meaning, but a site where the articulation of meaning – variable meaning(s) – can be made. And because 'texts' are 'multi-accentual', they can be articulated with different 'accents' by different people in different contexts for different politics. In this way, then, meaning, and the field of culture more generally, is always a site of negotiation and conflict; an arena in which hegemony may be won or lost (Hall 1998).

The introduction of hegemony into British cultural studies also produced a rethinking of the concept of popular culture itself (Hall 1996a, Storey 2009a, 2010). This rethinking involved bringing into active relationship two previously dominant but antagonistic ways of thinking about popular culture. The first tradition viewed popular culture as a culture imposed by the capitalist culture industries; a culture provided for profit and ideological manipulation (i.e. the Frankfurt School, structuralism, some versions of post-structuralism, political economy). This is popular culture as 'structure'. The second tradition saw popular culture as a culture spontaneously emerging from below; an 'authentic' folk, working-class or subculture – the 'voice' of the people (i.e. some versions of culturalism, social history and 'history from below'). This is popular culture as 'agency'. From the perspective of the cultural studies appropriation of hegemony, however, popular culture is neither an 'authentic' folk, working-class or subculture, nor a culture simply imposed by the capitalist culture industries, but a 'compromise equilibrium' (Gramsci 1971) between the two; a contradictory mix of forces from both 'below' and 'above'; both 'commercial' and 'authentic', marked by both 'resistance' and 'incorporation', 'structure' and 'agency'. Therefore, although a primary interest for cultural studies is the investigation of how people make culture from and with the commodities made available by the capitalist culture industries, working with the concept of hegemony is always to insist that such research should never lose sight of the conditions of existence which both enable and constrain practices of consumption. In every decade in the history of cultural studies the point has been repeatedly made. It is the 'Gramscian insistence', before (Storey 2009a, 2010), with and after Gramsci, learned from Marx (Marx 1977), that we make culture and we are made by culture; there is agency and there is structure. It is not enough to celebrate agency; nor is it enough to detail the structure(s) of power; we must always keep in mind the dialectical play between agency and structure, between production and consumption. A consumer, situated in a specific social context, always confronts a 'text' in its material existence as a result of particular conditions of production. But in the same way, a 'text' is confronted by a consumer, situated in a specific social context, who appropriates as culture, and 'produces in use' the range of possible meanings the 'text' can be made to bear – these cannot just be read off from the materiality of a 'text', or from the means or relations of its production (Hall 1980, Morley 1980, Du Gay et al. 1997). Working with hegemony may at times appear to lead to a certain celebration of the lived cultures of working people, but such celebration is always made in the full knowledge that what in one context is 'resistance' can become in another 'incorporation' (Storey 1999, 2009a, 2010).

Whereas the appropriation of Gramsci usually leads to a focus on the relations between production and consumption, the deployment of Foucault tends to generate work on representation, especially on the 'productive' nature of representation. Cultural studies takes a constructionist approach to representation (Hall 1997). Because things do not signify by themselves, what they mean has to be 'represented' in and through culture. That is, representation (through processes of description, conceptualisation and substitution) constructs the meaning of what is represented. The world certainly exists outside representation, but it is only in representations that

5

the world can be made meaningful. Representation is, therefore, a practice through which we make reality meaningful and through which we share and contest meanings of ourselves, of each other, and of the world.

If meaning is not something fixed and guaranteed in nature, but is the result of particular ways of representing nature in culture, then the meaning of something can never be fixed, final or true; its meaning will only ever be contextual and contingent and, moreover, always open to the changing relations of power. From a Foucauldian perspective (as developed in British cultural studies), representation always takes place in a discourse, which organises what can and cannot be said about a particular 'text'. Again, this is not to deny that the world exists in all its materiality but to insist that it is made meaningful in discourse (Foucault 1972). Meaning is made in discourses and, moreover, it is here that 'power produces knowledge . . . power and knowledge directly imply one another . . . there is no power relation without the correlative constitution of a field of knowledge, nor any knowledge that does not presuppose and constitute at the same time power relations' (Foucault 1979: 27). Dominant ways of knowing the world – making it meaningful – produced by those with the power to make their ways of knowing circulate discursively in the world, generate 'regimes of truth' (Foucault 2001a), which come to assume an authority over the ways in which we think and act; that is, provide us with 'subject positions' from which meanings can be made and actions carried out (Foucault 2001b). Cultural studies (following Foucault) seeks to discover 'how men [and women] govern (themselves and others) by the production of truth (. . . the establishment of domains in which the practice of true and false can be made at once ordered and pertinent)' (Foucault 2001a: 230). The power entangled in representation, therefore, is not a negative force, it is productive: 'We must cease once and for all to describe the effects of power in negative terms: it "excludes", it "represses", it "censors", it "abstracts", it "masks", it "conceals". In fact, power produces; it produces reality; it produces domains of objects and rituals of truth' (Foucault 1979: 194). This makes representation a key concept in cultural studies' focus on the relations between culture and power.

MORE ABOUT THIS BOOK

My aim, as stated earlier, is to present a range of theories and methods which have been used within cultural studies to study contemporary popular culture. In the main, I have tried to keep criticisms of the theories and methods to a minimum. I have, therefore, tried to avoid 'opinion writing', where, instead of explaining a theory or method, the author continually clutters his or her account with talk of problems and how he or she would solve them or would do the whole thing differently. There is, of course, a place for such an approach, but I am not convinced that the appropriate place is an introductory text. I would like the reader to take from this book an understanding of a range of significant theories and methods, rather than an understanding of what I think about them. Now it may, at times, become obvious what I think, but this should not be the primary knowledge that the reader takes from the book. For much the same reasons, I have quoted more than would be appropriate in a more 'advanced' text. But I feel quite strongly that introductory texts work best when they give their readers reasonable access to the theories and theorists under discussion.

I am also aware that I have simplified the field. Selection always means exclusion; and I know that my selection will not meet with universal approval. There are other valuable theories and methods which I have not discussed. In my defence, I can say only that it is not possible in a book of this size to cover all the theories and methods which have influenced cultural studies or which form part of its very structure. I have, however, selected the approaches which *I* believe are most significant.

In conclusion, it is difficult to do full justice to the complexities of the theories and methods that I have discussed. Really to do justice to the range and diversity of the study of contemporary popular culture within cultural studies would be the work of more than one book. Finally, whatever else this book is, it is certainly not intended as a substitute for reading firsthand the theories and methods discussed.

NOTES

1. For a fuller version of this history, with particular reference to popular culture, see Storey 2009b, 1999, 2009a, and 2003.
2. See Storey 2009a.
3. John Frow and Meaghan Morris offer this very useful definition of 'text' in cultural studies:

> There is a precise sense in which cultural studies uses the concept of text as its fundamental model . . . Rather than designating a place where meanings are constructed in a single level of inscription (writing, speech, film, dress . . .), it works as an interleaving of 'levels'. If a shopping mall [for example] is conceived on the model of textuality, then this 'text' involves practices, institutional structures and the complex forms of agency they entail, legal, political, and financial conditions of existence, and particular flows of power and knowledge, as well as a particular multilayered semantic organisation; it is an ontologically mixed entity, and one for which there can be no privileged or 'correct' reading. It is this, more than anything else, that forces cultural studies' attention to the diversity of audiences for or users of the structures of textuality it analyses – that is, to the open-ended social life of texts – and that forces it, thereby, to question the authority or finality of its own readings. (1996: 355–6)

   Frow and Morris make clear, texts exist only within networks of intertextual relations. To study a 'text' means to locate it across a range of competing moments of inscription, representation and struggle. In other words, cultural studies seeks to keep in equilibrium the different moments of cultural production – material production, symbolic production, textual production, and the 'production in use' of cultural consumption.
4. A major source of Hall's development of hegemony and articulation is Laclau and Mouffe (1985, 2009).

2

TELEVISION

Television is *the* popular cultural form of the twentieth and twenty-first centuries. It is without doubt the world's most popular leisure activity. On the day you are reading this book, there will be around the world in excess of 3.5 billion hours spent watching television (Kubey and Csikszentmihalyi 1990: 1). British audiences, for example, spend on average more than one-third of their waking hours watching television. In the USA, average time spent viewing is about twice as much (Allen 1992: 13). The 'average' American will spend in excess of seven years watching television (Kubey and Csikszentmihalyi 1990: xi).

ENCODING AND DECODING TELEVISUAL DISCOURSE

If we are in search of a founding moment when cultural studies first emerges from left-Leavisism, 'pessimistic' versions of Marxism, American mass communication models, culturalism and structuralism, the publication of Stuart Hall's 'Encoding and Decoding in the Television Discourse' (Hall 1980; first published in 1973) is perhaps it.[1]

In Hall's model of televisual communication (see Figure 1), the circulation of 'meaning' in televisual discourse passes through three distinctive moments: 'each has its specific modality and conditions

9

of existence' (128). First, media professionals put into meaningful televisual discourse their particular account of a 'raw' social event. At this moment in the circuit, a range of ways of looking at the world ('ideologies') are 'in dominance'.

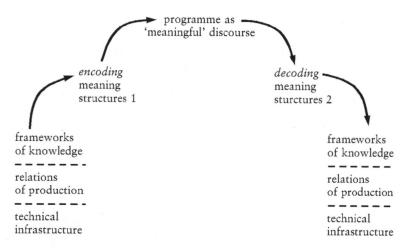

Figure 1

> [The moment of media production] is framed throughout by meanings and ideas; knowledge-in-use concerning the routines of production, historically defined technical skills, professional ideologies, institutional knowledge, definitions and assumptions, assumptions about the audience and so on frame the constitution of the programme through this production structure. Further, though the production structures of television originate the television discourse, they do not constitute a closed system. They draw topics, treatments, agendas, events, personnel, images of the audience, 'definitions of the situation' from other sources and other discursive formations within the wider socio-cultural and political structure of which they are a differentiated part. (129)

Thus the media professionals involved determine how the 'raw' social event will be encoded in discourse. However, in the second moment, once the 'raw' social event is in meaningful discourse, that is, once it has taken the form of televisual discourse, the formal rules of language and discourse are 'in dominance'; the message is now open, for example, to the play of polysemy.

> Since the visual discourse translates a three-dimensional world into two-dimensional planes, it cannot, of course, *be* the referent or concept it signifies . . . Reality exists outside language, but it is constantly mediated by and through language: and what we can know and say has to be produced in and through discourse. Discursive 'knowledge' is the product not of the transparent representation of the 'real' in language but of the articulation of language on real relations and conditions. Thus there is no intelligible discourse without the operation of a code. (131)

Finally, in the third moment, the moment of audience decoding, another range of ways of looking at the world ('ideologies') are 'in dominance'. An audience is confronted not by a 'raw' social event, but by a discursive translation of the event. If the event is to become 'meaningful' to the audience, it must decode and make sense of the discourse. 'If no "meaning" is taken, there can be no "consumption". If the meaning is not articulated in practice, it has no effect' (128). If an audience acts upon its decoding, this then becomes itself a social practice, a 'raw' social event, available to be encoded in another discourse. Thus, through the circulation of discourse, 'production' becomes 'consumption' to become 'production' again. The circuit starts in the 'social' and ends, to begin again, in the 'social'.

In other words, meanings and messages are not simply 'transmitted', they are always produced: first by the encoder from the 'raw' material of everyday life; second, by the audience in relation to its location in other discourses. Each moment is 'determinate', operating in its own conditions of production. Moreover, as Hall makes clear, the moments of encoding and decoding may not be perfectly symmetrical. There is nothing inevitable about the outcome of the process – what is intended and what is taken may not coincide. Media professionals may wish decoding to correspond with encoding, but they cannot prescribe or guarantee this. Governed by different conditions of existence, encoding and decoding are open to variable reciprocity. There is always the possibility of 'misunderstanding'.

> No doubt misunderstandings of a literal kind do exist. The viewer does not know the terms employed, cannot follow the complex logic of argument or exposition, is unfamiliar with the language, finds the concepts too alien or difficult or is foxed by the expository narrative. But more often broadcasters are concerned that the audience has failed to take the meaning as they – the broadcasters – intended. What they really mean to say is that viewers are not operating within the 'dominant' or 'preferred' code. (135)

It is this second 'misunderstanding' which interests Hall. Drawing on the work of sociologist Frank Parkin (1971), he suggests 'three hypothetical positions from which decodings of a televisual discourse may be constructed' (136). The first position he calls 'the dominant-hegemonic position' (136). This occurs '[w]hen the viewer takes the connoted meaning from, say, a television newscast or current affairs programme full and straight, and decodes the message in terms of the reference code in which it has been encoded, we might say that the viewer *is operating inside the dominant code*' (136). To decode a television discourse in this way is to be in harmony with the 'professional code' of the broadcasters.

> The professional code is 'relatively independent' of the dominant code, in that it applies criteria and transformational operations of its own, especially those of a technico-practical nature. The professional code, however, operates *within* the 'hegemony' of the dominant code. Indeed, it serves to reproduce the dominant definitions precisely by bracketing their hegemonic quality and operating instead with displaced professional codings which foreground such apparently neutral-technical questions as visual quality, news and presentational values, televisual quality, 'professionalism' and so on. (136)

The dominant code is always articulated through the professional code. David Morley (1980) gives the example of the way in which *Nationwide* reported the release of Patrick Meehan in 1976.[2]

> What is 'not relevant' as far as they are concerned is the whole political background to the case. Now that is not to say that this is a straightforwardly ideological decision to block out the political implications of the case. It's much more, in their terms, a communicative decision, as it appears to them; that is their notion of 'good television', to deal in that kind of 'personal drama'. (152)

The second decoding position is 'the negotiated code or position' (Hall 1980: 137). This is probably the majority position.

> Decoding within the negotiated version contains a mixture of adaptive and oppositional elements: it acknowledges the legitimacy of the hegemonic definitions to make the grand significations (abstract), while, at a more restricted, situational (situated) level, it makes its own ground rules – it operates with exceptions to the rule. It accords the privileged position to the dominant definitions of events while reserving the right to make a more negotiated application to 'local conditions', to its own *corporate* positions. This negotiated version of the dominant ideology is thus shot through with contradictions, though these are only on certain occasions brought to full visibility. (137)

An example of the negotiated code might be a worker who agrees in general terms with the news report's claim that increased wages cause inflation, while insisting on his or her right to strike for better pay and conditions.

Finally, the third position identified by Hall is 'the oppositional code'. This is the position occupied by the viewer who recognises the preferred code of the televisual discourse but who nonetheless chooses to decode within an alternative frame of reference. 'This is the case [for example] of the viewer who listens to a debate on the need to limit wages but "reads" every mention of the "national interest" as "class interest" ' (138).

Hall acknowledges that his hypothetical decoding positions 'need to be empirically tested and refined' (136). This in part is the project of David Morley's *The 'Nationwide' Audience* (1980) – to test Hall's model, to see how individual interpretations of televisual texts relate to 'social position'. Morley provides a useful summary (and clarification of) his own working understanding of Hall's encoding/decoding model as follows:

> 1. The production of a meaningful message in the TV discourse is always problematic 'work'. The same event can be encoded in more than one way. The study here is, then, of how and why certain production practices and structures tend to produce certain messages, which embody their meanings in certain recurring forms.
> 2. The message in social communication is always complex in structure and form. It always contains more than one potential 'reading'. Messages propose and prefer certain readings over others, but they can never become wholly closed around one reading. They remain polysemic.
> 3. The activity of 'getting meaning' from the message is also a problematic practice, however transparent and 'natural' it may seem. Messages encoded one way can always be read in a different way. (10)

Morley arranged for twenty-nine different groups to view two episodes (from 1976 and 1977) of the BBC's early-evening magazine/news programme *Nationwide*. The first programme was shown to eighteen groups, the second to eleven. Each group consisted of five to ten people. The groups were selected on the basis that they might be expected to differ in their decodings from 'dominant' to 'negotiated' to 'oppositional'.

Morley analysed the different readings produced by each group. Much of what he found seemed to confirm Hall's model (see Figure 2 for Morley's diagrammatic presentation of his findings). For example, a group of university arts students and a group of teacher-training-college students produced readings which moved between 'negotiated' and 'dominant', while the group of shop stewards produced an 'oppositional reading'.[3] However, when

14

the middle-class bank managers and the working-class apprentices both produced dominant readings, the correlation between class and reading position looked less secure, forcing Morley to acknowledge that decodings are not determined 'directly from social class position'. Rather, as he reformulates it: 'it is always a question of how social position *plus* particular discourse positions produce specific readings; readings which are structured because the structure of access to different discourses is determined by social position' (134).

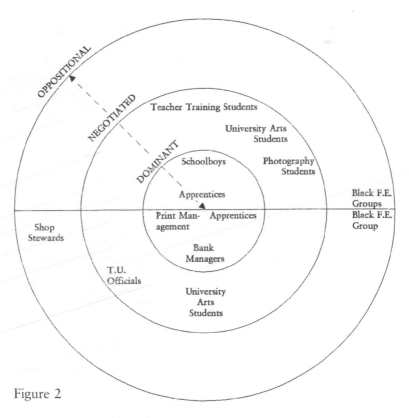

Figure 2

Morley, therefore, is able to explain the similarity in decodings between the working-class apprentices and the middle-class bank managers in terms of the formulation: determination of class plus other discourses (bodies of ideas and shared socio-cultural practices which help constitute us as social subjects and thus shape how we see and think about the world). Thus when we are 'interpellated' by a text, this is always in a context of other interpellations.[4]

The text–reader encounter does not occur in a moment isolated from other discourses, but always in a field of many discourses, some in harmony with the text, some which are in contradiction with it. One may read, for example, as a student, a Catholic, a socialist and a member of a youth subculture. Each discourse may pull us in a different direction. Each may assume a different level of importance in any given social setting. The response of the black Further Education students and other predominantly black groups to *Nationwide* – their 'critique of silence' – is therefore not to be explained as a failure of communication (the technical inability of the encoders to get their message across). Rather, what it demonstrates is the discourses of the text coming into conflict with the discourses of the reader. 'Here', as Morley explains 'the action of the cultures and discourses which these groups are involved in acts to block or inflect their interpellation by the discourse of *Nationwide*' (143). The converse is also evident in the decodings made by the working-class apprentices. 'Here it is not simply a case of the absence of "contradictory" discourses; rather it is the presence of other discourses which work in parallel with those of the programme – enabling these groups to produce "corresponding" representations' (143). Other discourses are always in play, 'although their action is more visible when it is a case of negative-contradictory rather than positive-reinforcing effect' (144). As Morley explains:

> [T]he social subject is always interpellated by a number of discourses, some of which are in parallel and reinforce each other, some of which are contradictory and block or inflect the successful interpellation of the subject by other discourses. Positively or negatively, other discourses are always involved in the relation of text and subject, although their action is simply more visible when it is a negative and

16

contradictory rather than a positive and reinforcing effect. (162)

However, despite these other determinations (these other discourses), Morley still stresses the importance of class in that it determines access (or the nature of access) to different discourses. As he explains, 'the subject's position in the social formation structures his or her range of access to various discourses and ideological codes' (158). This then explains the correlation between the readings made by the bank managers and the apprentices. The bank managers produced a dominant reading because of their political commitment to the conservatism of *Nationwide*'s discourse, while the apprentices accepted it uncritically because of a lack (unlike the shop stewards) of an alternative political discourse. Class was the key to both readings. The first was made on the basis of 'class interest', the second on the basis of the 'class interest' of the British education system (the working-class apprentices were schooled to be politically uncritical).

In the 'Afterword' to *The 'Nationwide' Audience*, Morley sums up (rather too modestly, in my opinion) the achievements of his research:

> I have been able to do no more than to indicate some of the ways in which social position and (sub)cultural frameworks may be related to individual readings. To claim more than that, on the basis of such a small sample, would be misleading. Similarly, I would claim only to have shown the viability of an approach which treats the audience as a set of cultural groupings rather than as a mass of individuals or as a set of rigid socio-demographic categories. Clearly, more work needs to be done on the relation between group and individual readings. (163)

Regretting the absence from his research of any discussion of how the context of decoding might enable and constrain the decodings produced, Morley's next research (1986) was an exploration of television viewing in the family home.[5]

Morley makes the point that:

> Once one takes seriously the fact that television is a domestic medium (and is characterised by programme forms specifically designed for that purpose), it becomes clear that the domestic context of television viewing is not some secondary factor, which can subsequently be sketched in. Rather, the domestic context of TV viewing, it becomes clear, is constitutive of its meaning. (1995: 321)

It had originally been Morley's intention to follow up his investigation of the Nationwide audience by conducting further interviews with the interviewees in the more 'natural' environment of their families and the home. Limitations of time and a lack of funding combined to ensure that this did not happen. In a way, then, it could be argued that *Family Television* represents to a certain extent the 'completion' of the *Nationwide* research project. Specifically, what Morley seeks to accomplish in this research is to bring into a critical and fruitful relationship questions which until then had generally been kept apart, seen as the separate provinces of different disciplinary approaches – how television is interpreted (literary/ semiological approaches) and how television is used (sociological approaches). The combination 'the respective strengths of these two different perspectives', enabled him, he argues, 'to consider problems of audience decoding/choice in the context of family leisure' (1986: 13). Moreover, by locating the audience in a domestic context, he is able to demonstrate the ways in which the cultural consumption of television always involves so much more than isolated individuals making particular interpretations of specific programmes. As he explains:

> 'Watching television' cannot be assumed to be a one-dimensional activity which has equivalent meaning or significance at all times for all who perform it. I was concerned to identify and investigate the differences hidden behind the catch-all description 'watching television'; both the differences between

the choices made by different kinds of viewers in relation to different viewing options, and the differences (of attention and comprehension) between different viewers' responses to the same viewing materials – differences which are masked by the finding that they all 'watched' a given programme. (1986: 16)

Watching television is always so much more than a series of acts of interpretation; it is above all else a social practice. That is, it can be a means both to isolate oneself (Don't talk to me, I'm watching this), or to make contact with other family members (watching a programme you are indifferent about, or worse, in order to make contact with a particular member of the family or the family as a whole). It can also be a means to reward or punish children (You cannot watch Y until you've done X). In these ways, the consumption of television is as much about social relationships as it is about interpretations of individual programmes. The German media theorist Hermann Bausinger provides an example of a woman's account of her husband's behaviour: ' "Early in the evening we watch very little TV. Only when my husband is in a real rage. He comes home, hardly says anything and switches on the TV." ' Although, as Bausinger observes, 'this is a direct expression of his psychic state, which is . . . habitualized and routinized, the specific semantic of the everyday comes in: pushing the button doesn't signify, "I would like to watch this", but rather, "I would like to hear and see nothing" ' (1984: 344). Contrary to the myth, that this example might seem to support, that watching television kills conversation, Bausinger in fact argues that 'Media contents are materials for conversation' (350). Watching television (and this is also true with other media), actually generates a common currency (television talk) to be exchanged in the cultural economy of everyday life. Television discourse is not just a currency which operates in the family, it is also important in most of the everyday interactions between people. As one respondent told Morley about television discourse at work: 'We haven't got much else in common, so we talk a lot about TV' (1986: 79). In this way, rather than an alternative to a social life, the consumption of television may play an integral part in its success. In certain instances, not being able to deal in the currency of television talk (i.e. not having seen particular programmes) may put a person at a distinct social disadvantage in the workplace or with a specific peer group. As Morley maintains:

> [T]elevision can be seen to provide in one sense an alibi, in another sense a context, for encounters between family members, where the content of the television programme they are watching together may often simply serve as a common experiential ground for conversation. In this kind of instance, television is being used as a focus, as a method for engaging in social interaction with others. So, far from simply disrupting family interaction, television is being used purposefully by family members to construct the occasions of their interactions, and to construct the context within which they can interact. It is being used to provided the reference points, the ground, the material, the stuff of conversation. (22)

In the introduction to *Crossroads: The Drama of a Soap Opera*, Dorothy Hobson observes, '[I]t is only by long and relaxed talks and viewing *with* the audience that any understanding of how people watch television can be achieved. The effort is well worth while for it reveals the important contribution which viewers make to any television programme which they watch' (1982: 12). Hobson's account of the consumption of the British soap opera *Crossroads* forms only a small part of her study of the production of the programme. Nevertheless, her observations have a formative place in the development of 'ethnographic' work in (British) cultural studies. Hobson conducted a series of unstructured interviews with viewers of the programme, mostly women, after watching episodes with them in their homes. As she explains, 'It is important to stress that the interviews were unstructured because I wanted the viewers to determine what was interesting or what they noticed, or liked, or disliked about the programme and specifically about the episodes which we had watched' (105).

Although her book does not seek to articulate a precise theoretical position, the research which informs it is nonetheless structured by clear underlying assumptions about the productive work of audiences. As she explains:

> Different people watch television programmes for different reasons, and make different 'readings' of those programmes, and much of what they say is determined by preconceived ideas and opinions which they bring to a programme. The message is not solely in the 'text' but can be changed or 'worked on' by the audience as they make their own interpretation of a programme. (105–6)

Watching *Crossroads* with its audience allowed Hobson to understand the extent to which 'Watching television is part of the everyday life of viewers. It is not, as is sometimes suggested, a separate activity undertaken in perfect quiet in comfortable surroundings' (110). Television is usually watched in the midst of other everyday activities. As Hobson discovered, domestic routines and responsibilities and the expectations of other family members, ensured that many of the women with whom she watched *Crossroads* were not allowed the luxury of the detailed concentration expected and enjoyed by staff and students watching in darkened rooms on media studies courses. As she quickly was made aware, domestic circumstances impact on both the level of concentration with which, and the perspective from which, a programme is viewed. As she explains, 'To watch a programme at meal time with the mother of young children is an entirely different experience from watching with a seventy-two-year-old widow whose day is largely structured around television programmes' (111).

Meaning is not, as Hobson discovered, something which happens only once, in the first moment of consumption as one sits in front of the television screen. The making of meaning is an ongoing process which may reach well beyond the first moment of consumption. New contexts will bring about the enactment of new significances; a narrative seemingly discarded seems suddenly to have a new relevance and a new utility. Travelling on a train back from London, Hobson discovered how viewers can integrate and reintegrate the world of soap opera, for example, into their own lives: playing a 'fantastical' game in which the fictional and the real are allowed to merge. She recounts how she overheard, during the course of that train journey, a conversation between four pensioners in which they talked about their respective children and grandchildren, and then without comment, the conversation switched to a discussion about the current problems of a character in the British soap opera *Coronation Street* (125). She listened as the four women discussed recent happenings in the soap opera and interwove these with a discussion of recent narratives in their own family lives; family narratives then in turn provoked further discussion of soap opera narratives; soap opera narratives then provoked more discussion of family narratives. And so it went on.

Hobson's research also reveals the extent to which viewers use their own experience to measure and judge the events happening in television programmes like *Crossroads*. On the basis of these findings, she dismisses as 'invalid' the common claim that the appeal of soap opera is escapism. Soap operas, she maintains, 'are precisely a way of understanding and coping with problems which are recognised as "shared" by other women, both in the programme and in "real life"' (131). What is important, what the women she interviewed sought to relate to, is the raising of social problems, regardless of the adequacy or the supposed progressiveness of the programme's narrative solutions. As one women told Hobson, in response to a question about *Crossroads*' failure to pursue an issue to a radical conclusion, 'you can make your own conclusions' (132). Hobson insists that viewers 'work with the text and add their own experiences and opinions to the stories in the programme' (135). People

> do not sit there watching and taking it all in without any mental activity or creativity . . . they expect to contribute to the production which they are watching and bring their own knowledge to augment the text. Stories which seem too fantastic for an everyday serial are transformed through a sympathetic audience reading whereby they strip the storyline to the idea behind it and construct an understanding on the skeleton that is left. (135–6)

I think Hobson is absolutely correct to point to the creativity of the audience for *Crossroads*; where I disagree with her is about the extent of its creativity. She claims, 'To try to say what *Crossroads* means to its audience is impossible for there is no single *Crossroads*, there are as many different *Crossroads* as there are viewers' (136). Later, she adds, 'there can be as many interpretations of a programme as the individual viewers bring to it. There is no overall intrinsic message or meaning in the work, but it comes alive and communicates when the viewers add their own interpretation and understanding to the programme' (170). Against these claims, I would want to insist on two points of objection. First, it is undoubtedly the case that programmes have material structures, which must set definite limits on the range and possibilities of interpretation. Second, viewers always view in contexts, both social and discursive, and these must set definite limits on the range and possibilities of interpretation. For these reasons, I think Hobson is wrong to propose, what is in effect, an entirely subjective theory of interpretation. Moreover, I think it is the case that her own excellent study of women watching *Crossroads* contradicts this theoretical claim.

In another interesting piece of work based on interviews with a woman working as a sales manager in a telephone sales office, Hobson develops the ideas she had first formulated on the train journey back from London. On the basis of this new research she argues that 'women use television programmes as part of their general discourse on their own lives, the lives of their families and friends and to add interest to their working lives' (1990: 62). Her research highlights how quickly a conversation about a television programme can become a conversation about the lives and interests of the women involved. For example, discussion of events in a soap opera can produce a discussion about events in the real lives of viewers. In this way, Hobson maintains, viewers are able to use events within television narratives to explore issues in their own lives; issues that might otherwise remain too painful to speak about openly in public. She argues that recognition of how women use television in this way should disprove the theory that watching television is a mindless, passive event in the lives of the viewers. On the contrary, the events and subjects covered in television programmes often acted as the catalyst for wide-ranging and open discussions. The communication was extended far beyond the moment of viewing. (1990: 66)

As she concludes, 'It is the interweaving of the narratives of fiction with the narratives of their reality that formed the basis for sharing their experiences and opinions and *creating their own culture* within their workplace' (my italics; 71). Making a similar point, Mary Ellen Brown argues that such conversations illustrate what she calls 'a carnivalesque sense of play in the crossing of the boundary between fiction and reality' (1990: 195). Furthermore, Brown maintains that women's talk about soap operas is best understood as a fundamental part of the long tradition of women's oral culture – a 'feminine discourse' (183). As she explains:

> As consumers of soap operas and the products they advertise, women do participate in the process of consumption, but the extent to which women can be said to be the passive objects or 'victims' of dominant discursive practices by watching and enjoying soap operas is limited by the women's use of these same cultural forms to affirm their own positions of subjectivity in a women's discursive tradition. This breaking of the rules is a source of pleasure, and the act of taking that pleasure entails defiance of dominant reading practices which attempt to shape the construction of meaning in our culture. Because the hierarchy of dominant values is either ignored or parodied in some of the reading practices around soaps, these practices may open up new possibilities for ways of thinking about culture from the subordinate's point of view. (198)

As both Hobson and Brown remind us, what we might call 'television talk' is not just talk about what is on, has been on, or is coming on television, it is also talk provoked by television. Tamar Liebes and Elihu Katz provide the example of a Russian who had recently emigrated to Israel and said that 'viewing [the American soap opera] *Dallas* is like doing homework for other conversations' (1993: 92). As Liebes and Katz also observe:

> Viewing escapist programs is not as escapist as it seems. In fact, viewers typically use television fiction as a forum for discussing their own lives. Concern over family, social issues, women's status, etc. are activated in response to these programs ... and there is good reason to believe that an agenda is set for discussion as a result of the negotiation between the culture of the viewers and of the producers. (154)

One obvious example of this is the way in which discussion of the relationship difficulties of a particular fictional character can quickly provide the pretext and the context for revelations about real difficulties in real relationships. Talking about the problems of a character can be a rather less painful or less embarrassing way of talking about one's own problems or a relatively easy means to introduce these problems into a discussion. Moreover, as John Fiske observes, television talk provides cultural studies researchers with an important bridge between the social and the textual, replete, as it is, with 'clues about which meanings offered by the text are being mobilised' in people's everyday lived cultures (1989c: 66).

TELEVISION AND 'THE IDEOLOGY OF MASS CULTURE'

In the early 1980s, the Dutch cultural critic Ien Ang placed the following advertisement in *Viva*, a Dutch women's magazine: 'I like watching the TV serial *Dallas*, but often get odd reactions to it. Would anyone like to write and tell me why you like watching it too, or dislike it? I should like to assimilate these reactions in my university thesis. Please write to . . .' (1985: 10). The context for Ang's research was the emergence of the American 'prime-time soap' *Dallas* as an international success (watched in over ninety countries) in the early 1980s. In the Netherlands, *Dallas* was regularly watched by 52 per cent of the population.

Following the advertisement, Ang received forty-two letters (thirty-nine from women or girls) from both lovers and haters of *Dallas*. These form the empirical basis of her study of the pleasure(s) of watching *Dallas* for its predominantly female audience. For Ang's letter-writers; the pleasure or displeasures of *Dallas* are inextricably linked with questions of 'realism'. The extent to which a letter-writer finds the programme 'good' or 'bad' is determined by whether they find it 'realistic' (good) or 'unrealistic' (bad). Critical of both 'empiricist realism' (a text is considered realistic to the extent it adequately reflects that which exists outside itself) and 'classic realism' (Colin McCabe's 1974 claim that realism is an illusion created by the extent to which a text can successfully conceal its constructedness), Ang contends that *Dallas* is best understood as an example of what she calls 'emotional realism'. Accordingly, *Dallas* can be read on two levels: the level of denotation (the literal content of the programme, general storyline, character interactions, etc.) and the level of connotation (the associations and implications which resonate from the storyline and character interactions, etc.).

> It is striking; the same things, people, relations and situations which are regarded at the denotative level as unrealistic, and unreal, are at the connotative level apparently not seen at all as unreal, but in fact as 'recognizable'. Clearly, in the connotative reading process the denotative level of the text is put in brackets. (42)

Viewing *Dallas*, like any other programme, is a selective process, reading across the text from denotation to connotation, weaving our sense of self in and out of the narrative. As one letter-writer says, 'Do you know why I like watching it? I think it's because those problems and intrigues, the big and little pleasures and troubles occur in our own lives too . . . In real life I know a horror like J. R., but he's just an ordinary builder' (43). It is this ability to connect our own lives with the lives of a family of Texan millionaires which gives the programme its emotional realism. We may not be rich, but we have other fundamental things in common: relationships and broken relationships, happiness and sadness, illness and health. Those who find it realistic shift the focus of attention from the particularity of the (denotative) narrative to the generality of its (connotative) themes.

26

Given the way that *Dallas* plays with the emotions in an endless game of musical chairs in which happiness inevitably gives way to misery, Ang calls this a 'tragic structure of feeling' (46). As one letter-writer told her, 'Sometimes I really enjoy having a good cry with them. And why not? In this way my other bottled-up emotions find an outlet' (49). Viewers who 'escape' in this way are not so much engaging in 'a denial of reality as playing with it . . . [in a] game that enables one to place the limits of the fictional and the real under discussion, to make them fluid. And in that game an imaginary participation in the fictional world is experienced as pleasurable' (49). Whatever else is involved, part of the pleasure of *Dallas* is quite clearly connected to the amount of fluidity which viewers are able or willing to establish between its fictional world and the world of their day-to-day existence. But how does *Dallas* construct this tragic structure of feeling? Ang's answer is that it is 'the combination of melodramatic elements and the narrative structure of soap opera that evokes a tragic structure of feeling' (78). In order to activate this structure of feeling, it is necessary to have the cultural capital to take up a reading formation informed by what she calls (following Peter Brooks 1976) the 'melodramatic imagination'. For the melodramatic imagination, everyday existence, with its pains and triumphs, its victories and defeats, is as profoundly meaningful and significant as the grand human suffering of classical tragedy. It offers a means of organising reality, cut loose from the certainties of religion, into meaningful contrasts and conflicts. As a narrative form committed to melodrama's emphatic contrasts, conflicts and emotional excess, *Dallas* is well placed to give sustenance to, and make manifest, the melodramatic imagination. For those who see the world in this way (Ang claims that it demands a cultural competence most often shared by women), 'the pleasure of *Dallas* . . . is not a *compensation* for the presumed drabness of daily life, nor a *flight* from it, but a *dimension* of it' (83).

The melodramatic imagination activates what is perceived in the text as a tragic structure of feeling, which in turn produces the pleasure of emotional realism. As the melodramatic imagination is in effect a 'reading formation' (see Chapter 3), it follows that not all viewers of *Dallas* will take up this particular reading position.

On the basis of the views expressed in the letters, Ang is able to separate the viewers into four reading positions connected by what she calls 'the ideology of mass culture' (15). The ideology articulates the view that popular culture is the result of capitalist commodity production and is therefore subject to the laws of the capitalist market economy; the result of which is the seemingly endless circulation of degraded commodities, whose only real significance is that they make a profit for their producers. The ideology of mass culture, like any ideological discourse, seeks to interpellate individuals into specific subject positions. The letters suggest four positions from which to consume *Dallas*: those who strongly dislike the programme; those whose pleasures are the result of ironical viewing; fans; populists.

The letter-writers who strongly dislike *Dallas* draw most clearly on the ideology. They use it in two ways: to locate the programme negatively as an example of 'mass culture', and as a means to account for and support their dislike of the programme. As Ang puts it, 'their reasoning boils down to this: "*Dallas* is obviously bad because it's mass culture, and that's why I dislike it" ' (95–6). In this way, the ideology both comforts and reassures: 'it makes a search for more detailed and personal explanations superfluous, because it provides a finished explanatory model that convinces, sounds logical and radiates legitimacy' (96). This is not to say that it is wrong to dislike *Dallas*, only that professions of dislike are often made without thinking – in fact, with a confidence born of uncritical thought.

Viewers who occupy the second position demonstrate how it is possible to like *Dallas* and still subscribe to the ideology of mass culture. The contradiction is resolved by 'mockery and irony' (97). *Dallas* is subjected to an ironising and mocking commentary in which it 'is transformed from a seriously intended melodrama to the reverse: a comedy to be laughed at. Ironising viewers therefore do not take the text as it presents itself, but invert its preferred meaning through ironic commentary' (98). From this position, the pleasure of *Dallas* derives from the fact that it is bad: pleasure and bad mass culture are reconciled in an instant. As one of the letter-writers puts it, 'Of course *Dallas* is mass culture and therefore bad, but precisely because I am so well aware of that I can really enjoy watching it and poke fun at it' (100). For both the ironising viewer and the hater of *Dallas*, the ideology of mass culture operates as a bedrock of common sense, making judgements obvious and self-evident. Although both operate within the normative standards of the ideology, the difference between the two positions is marked by the question of pleasure. On the one hand, the ironisers can have pleasure without guilt in the sure and declared knowledge that they know that mass culture is bad. On the other hand, the haters, although secure in the same knowledge, can, nevertheless, suffer 'a conflict of feelings if, *in spite of this*, they cannot escape its seduction' (101).

Thirdly, there are those who view as fans. For the viewers who occupy the previous two positions, actually to like *Dallas* without resort to irony is to be identified as someone duped by mass culture. As one letter-writer puts it, 'The aim is simply to rake in money, lots of money. And people try to do that by means of all these things – sex, beautiful people, wealth. And you always have people who fall for it' (103). The claim is presented with all the confidence of having the full weight of the ideology's discursive support. Ang analyses the different strategies which the fans of *Dallas* must use to deal consciously and unconsciously with such condescension. The first strategy is to 'internalise' the ideology; to acknowledge the 'dangers' of *Dallas*, but to declare one's ability to deal with them in order to derive pleasure from the programme. Another strategy is to confront the ideology of mass culture as this letter-writer does, 'Many people find it worthless or without substance. But I think it does have substance' (105). But, as Ang points out, the writer remains firmly within the discursive constraints of the ideology as she attempts to relocate *Dallas* in a different relationship to the binary oppositions with substance/without substance, good/bad. 'This letter-writer "negotiates' as it were within the discursive space created by the ideology of mass culture, she does not situate herself outside it and does not speak from an opposing ideological position' (106).

As Ang shows, the fans of *Dallas* find it necessary to locate their pleasure in relation to the ideology of mass culture; they 'internalise' the ideology; they 'negotiate' with the ideology; they use 'surface irony' to defend their pleasure against the withering dismissal of the ideology. What all these strategies of defence reveal is 'that there is no clear-cut ideological alternative which can be employed against the ideology of mass culture – at least no alternative that offsets the latter in power of conviction and coherence' (109–10). The struggle therefore, as so far described, between those who like *Dallas* and those who dislike it, is an unequal struggle between those who argue from within the discursive strength and security of the ideology of mass culture, and those who resist from within (for them) its inhospitable confines. 'In short, these fans do not seem to be able to take up an effective ideological position – an identity – from which they can say in a positive way and independently of the ideology of mass culture: "I like *Dallas* because . . ." ' (110).

The final viewing position as revealed in the letters (one that might help these fans) is one informed by the ideology of populism. At the core of this ideology is the belief that one person's taste is of equal value to another person's taste. As one letter-writer puts it, 'I find the people who react oddly rather ludicrous – they can't do anything about someone's taste. And anyway they might find things pleasant that you just can't stand seeing or listening to' (113). The ideology of populism insists that as taste is an autonomous category, continually open to individual inflection, it is absolutely meaningless to pass aesthetic judgements on other people's preferences. Given that this would seem to be an ideal ideology from which to defend one's pleasure in *Dallas*, why do so few of the letter-writers adopt it? Ang's answer is that it is to do with the ideology's extremely limited vocabulary. After one has repeated 'there's no accounting for taste' a few times, the argument begins to appear rather limited. Compared to this, the ideology of mass culture has an extensive and elaborate range of arguments and theories. Little wonder, then, that when invited to explain why they like or dislike *Dallas*, the letter-writers find it difficult to escape the normative ideological discourse of mass culture.

Cultural studies, especially feminist cultural studies, must, according to Ang, break with the ideology of mass culture. She sees pleasure as the key concept in a transformed feminist cultural

politics. Feminist cultural studies must struggle against 'the pater-
nalism of the ideology of mass culture . . . [in which w]omen are . . .
seen as the passive victims of the deceptive messages of soap operas
. . . [their] pleasure . . . totally disregarded' (118–19). Pleasure
should not be condemned as an obstruction to the feminist goal of
women's liberation. The question which Ang poses is: can pleasure
through identification with the women of 'women's weepies' or the
emotionally masochistic women of soap operas 'have a meaning for
women which is relatively independent of their political attitudes?'
(133). Her answer is yes: fantasy and fiction does

> not function in place of, but beside, other dimensions of life
> (social practice, moral or political consciousness). It . . . is
> a source of pleasure because it puts 'reality' in parenthesis,
> because it constructs imaginary solutions for real contra-
> dictions which in their fictional simplicity and their simple
> fictionality step outside the tedious complexity of the existing
> social relations of dominance and subordination. (135)

Of course this does not mean that representations of women do
not matter. They can still be condemned for being reactionary in
an ongoing cultural politics. But for women to experience pleasure from them is a completely different issue: '[I]t need not imply
that we are also bound to take up these positions and solutions in
our relations to our loved ones and friends, our work, our political
ideals and so on' (135).

> Fiction and fantasy, then, function by making life in the
> present pleasurable, or at least liveable, but this does not by
> any means exclude radical political activity or consciousness.
> It does not follow that feminists must not persevere in trying
> to produce new fantasies and fight for a place for them . . .
> It does, however, mean that, where cultural consumption is
> concerned, no fixed standard exists for gauging the 'progres-
> siveness' of a fantasy. The personal may be political, but the
> personal and the political do not always go hand in hand.
> (135–6)

31

THE TWO ECONOMIES OF TELEVISION

John Fiske (1987) argues that cultural commodities – including television – from which popular culture is made circulate in two simultaneous economies: the financial and the cultural. The financial economy is primarily concerned with exchange value, the cultural is primarily focused on use – 'meanings, pleasures, and social identities' (311). There is, of course, continual interaction between these separate but related economies. Fiske gives the example of *Hill Street Blues*. The programme was made by MTM and sold to NBC, which then made a sponsorship deal with Mercedes Benz – in effect making the audience for *Hill Street Blues* available to Mercedes Benz. This all happened in the financial economy. In the cultural economy, the series changed from a cultural commodity (to be sold to NBC) to a site for the production of meanings and pleasures for its audience. In the same way, the audience changed from commodity (to be sold to Mercedes Benz) to a producer of meanings and pleasures.

Fiske insists that 'the power of audiences-as-producers in the cultural economy is considerable' (313). The power of the audience 'derives from the fact that meanings do not circulate in the cultural economy in the same way that wealth does in the financial' (313). While it is possible to possess wealth, it is much harder to possess meanings and pleasures. In the cultural economy – unlike in the financial economy – commodities do not move in a linear fashion from production to consumption; pleasures and meanings circulate without any real distinction between production and consumption. Moreover, the power of the consumer becomes manifest in the failure of producers to predict what will sell. 'Twelve out of thirteen records fail to make a profit, TV series are axed by the dozen, expensive films sink rapidly into red figures (*Raise the Titanic* is an ironic example – it nearly sank the Lew Grade empire)' (313).

In an attempt to offset the failures, the culture industries produce 'repertoires' of goods in the hope of attracting an audience. But audiences constantly engage in what Fiske calls – borrowing from Michel de Certeau (1984) – 'semiotic guerilla warfare' (316). Whereas the culture industries seek to incorporate audiences as commodity consumers, the audience often excorporates a television text, for example, for its own purposes. Fiske cites the example of the way in which Australian Aboriginal viewers appropriated Rambo as a figure of resistance, relevant to their own political and cultural struggles. He also cites the example of Russian Jews watching *Dallas* in Israel and reading it as 'capitalism's self-criticism' (320).[6]

Fiske argues that resistance to the power of the powerful by those without power in Western societies takes two forms: semiotic and social. The first is mainly concerned with meanings, pleasures and social identities; the second, with transformations of the socio-economic system. He contends that 'the two are closely related, although relatively autonomous' (316). Popular culture operates mostly, 'but not exclusively', in the domain of semiotic power. It is involved in 'the struggle between homogenisation and difference, or between consensus and conflict' (316). In this sense, popular culture is a semiotic battlefield in which conflicts are fought out between the forces of incorporation and the forces of resistance, between imposed sets of meanings, pleasures and social identities, and the meanings, pleasures and social identities produced in acts of semiotic resistance: 'the hegemonic forces of homogeneity are always met by the resistances of heterogeneity' (Fiske 1989a: 8).

Fiske's two economies operate in the interests of opposing sides of the struggle: the financial economy tends to favour the forces of incorporation and homogenisation; while the cultural economy tends to favour the forces of resistance and difference. Semiotic resistance – in which dominant meanings are challenged by subordinate meanings – has the effect of undermining capitalism's attempt at ideological homogeneity. In this way, according to Fiske, the dominant class's 'intellectual and moral leadership' (Gramsci 2009: 75) is challenged.

Fiske's approach to popular culture – including television – is one which recognises popular culture as 'a site of struggle' and, while acknowledging 'the power of the forces of dominance', chooses instead to direct its attention to 'the popular tactics by which these forces are coped with, are evaded or are resisted'. In other words, '[i]nstead of tracing exclusively the processes of incorporation, it investigates rather that popular vitality and creativity that makes incorporation such a constant necessity' (20). Moreover, 'instead of concentrating on the omnipresent, insidious practices of the dominant ideology, it attempts to understand the everyday resistances and evasions that make that ideology work so hard and insistently to maintain itself and its values'. His approach 'is essentially optimistic, for it finds in the vigour and vitality of the people evidence both of the possibility of social change and of the motivation to drive it' (20–1).

NEW MEDIA, YOUTUBE AND POST-TELEVISION

The first thing we have to consider in a discussion of new media is an underlying debate that accompanies both positive and negative accounts of its social and cultural impact. What I mean is this: studies of new media are often haunted by debates about old media, in particular the influence of the work of Marshall McLuhan and Raymond Williams. The key distinction between these two positions is the question of the relationship between media and society. For McLuhan, media (understood in very broad terms) have the power to shape social behaviour and bring about radical cultural change. Against what he thought of as McLuhan's 'technological determinism', Williams argues that media (their meanings and uses) are shaped by existing social relationships.

According to McLuhan, human societies have moved through four stages, each organised around a particular mode of media:

1. oral communication;
2. hand-writing combined with oral communication;
3. print communication;
4. electronic communication. (McLuhan 1962, 1968).

What is called new media represents a further intensification of the fourth stage. The power of any media, so this argument goes, is its capacity to operate as an 'extension of ourselves' (1968: 15). Whereas print media is an extension of the eye, electronic media is an extension of the nervous system. Such prosthetic extensions, he claims, impact on 'the whole psychic and social complex' (1968: 11).[7] In other words, his claim is that such extensions affect both our consciousness and the social and cultural development of the societies in which we live. As he explains, 'Sense ratios change when any one sense or bodily or mental function is externalised in technological form' (1962: 24). Media content is, therefore, of little significance to McLuhan; as he famously claims 'the medium is the message' (1968: 15).

> The effects of technology do not occur at the level of opinions or concepts, but alter sense ratios or patterns of perception steadily and without any resistance. The serious artist is the only person able to encounter technology with impunity, just because he is an expert aware of the changes in sense perception. (1968: 27)

On the basis of this, McLuhan can be very dismissive of what we might think of as conventional media studies, with its focus on content, referring to what he calls 'the numb stance of the technological idiot. For the "content" of a medium is like the juicy piece of meat carried by the burglar to distract the watchdog of the mind' (1968: 26). As a consequence, he claims that the power and significance of a particular media 'has little to do with "content" ' (1968: 62). Furthermore, 'Societies have always been shaped more by the nature of the media by which men communicate than by the content of the communication' (McLuhan and Fiore 1967: 1). Although we might disagree with McLuhan's claim that content is merely a distraction, his argument does have the effect of making us take seriously the technological materiality of a media. Rather than see it simply as a delivery system, we are encouraged to see it as something that can enable and constrain changes in human consciousness and social relationships.

Williams (1990) takes a very different view of the relationship between media and society. Rather than see technology as determining its use and thus determining social change, Williams argues that the use and significance of any new technology, including all forms of media, is always determined by the social situation in which it emerges; this has a direct impact on how a technology influences social change. According to Williams, the influence of a new technology is always mediated through the power relations embedded in a particular social formation. Whereas for McLuhan a technology determines its use and its social effects, for Williams this will depend heavily on the nature of the social formation in which it emerges, and therefore, while influenced by existing structures of power, will always be unpredictable. In other words, Williams rejects totally McLuhan's argument that the mode of communication determines the shape and development of a social formation. For example, print communication did not determine the social relations of print culture, rather these emerged as a result of social struggles over who should be allowed to read and write. Take, for example, the development of literacy during the industrial revolution in Britain in the eighteenth and nineteenth centuries. Industrialisation required a more educated workforce than working the land had needed. This new requirement caused much debate within the dominant social classes. The result was that the new industrial working class were taught to read but not to write. This would enable them to read the rules and regulations of the new factory system and to read the Bible for its power of moral improvement and social reconciliation. Writing was seen as unnecessary to their menial status. But of course once enabled to read, the new industrial working class could read material more radical and encouraging of social change, and, moreover, they could learn to write. Therefore, the impact of print communications on social relations was heavily mediated by the existing power relation into which print technology emerged. Put simply, the invention of the printing press did not produce mass literacy; mass literacy, at least in the West, was the result of social and political struggles. The fundamental problem with technological determinism is that it situates the technology and its development as a self-generating force outside processes of social development and then claims that once in use, the technology will determine the future shape and development of social processes. However, to really understand the development and use of a new technology it has to be seen from its very beginnings as situated in processes of social development and enabled and constrained by forms of human agency and social structures. The use of a technology is not determined by the technology itself but by the social, economic and political circumstances in which the technology is produced and consumed. Like anything else (as we saw in Chapter 1), it is entangled in relations of culture and power.

Williams is not just critical of McLuhan for his formalism (the meaning of the technology is determined by the technology itself) but also because of the political implications of his technological determinism. According to Williams, McLuhan's approach 'ratifies the society and culture we now have . . . For if the medium – whether print or television – is the cause, all other causes, all that men ordinarily see as history, are at once reduced to effects' (127). Moreover, such an approach offers theoretical support to the prevailing structures of media and social power:

> If the effect of the medium is the same, whoever controls or uses it, and whatever apparent content he may try to insert, then we can forget ordinary political and cultural argument and let the technology run itself. It is hardly surprising that this conclusion has been welcomed by the 'media-men' of the existing institutions. . . . Thus what began as pure formalism, and as speculation on human essence, ends as operative social theory and practice, in the heartland of the most dominative and aggressive communications institutions in the world. (Williams 1990: 128)

I started this chapter with the claim that television is the popular cultural form of the twentieth and twenty-first centuries. However, there are signs that the hegemony of television's popularity may be coming to an end. The evidence for this change is found, for example, in the many new ways people consume television content - via new media forms such as the laptop and the mobile phone. It was once a commonplace to suggest that the television set had replaced the fireplace as the focal point in the family living room. Now that the visual content of television can be viewed on many different platforms, the days of the television set's domestic centrality may be over. Perhaps the final challenge to the centrality of television is the phenomenal success of YouTube; more than any other platform for visual content delivery, it is YouTube that perhaps justifies using the term post-television.

YouTube was founded by Chad Hurley, Steve Che, and Jawad Karim. The site was launched in June 2005. In October 2006 Google paid $1.65 billion for it. In November 2007 it was listed as the most popular website in the UK. From early 2008 it has been consistently in the global top ten of most visited websites (Burgess and Green 2009: 1-2). According to YouTube itself, 'People are watching hundreds of millions of videos a day on YouTube and uploading hundreds of thousands of videos daily. In fact ten hours of video is uploaded to YouTube every minute' (http://www.youtube.com/press_room, August 2009).

YouTube has attracted a great deal of critical attention since it first appeared in 2005. Initially it was regarded as a space of variety and strangeness. Early accounts always feeling obliged to list the curious diversity of what can be found there – from animals doing strange things to humans doing even stranger things. However, within a year of its emergence YouTube was being discussed in very serious terms: the first signs of a post-television age, a focus of serious media industry interest, the site of new and difficult legal issues and moral and ethical concerns. In simple terms, media discourses around YouTube ranged across a terrain of extremes: at one end there were endless stories about cyber-bullying and youth out of control or the decline of intellectual and moral authority, while at the other there were stories of a supposed democratic revolution in user-generated content (for an interesting critical discussion of the latter see Turner 2009).

When the site began its slogan was 'Your Digital Video Repository'. This was soon replaced by the slogan 'Broadcast Yourself'. It is the shift from the first to the second, from archive to imagined community, which captures some of the reasons for YouTube's incredible success. The content of the site comes from many sources, including non-professional video makers, large and small-to-medium media producers (television companies, advertising agencies, sports organisations, political parties), artists, political activists, citizen journalists, and fans. It is this complex and contradictory array of contributors and interests that makes YouTube 'a site of participatory culture' (Burgess and Green, 2009: vii). The YouTube community is a complex and contradictory community.

For non-professional video producers and others working outside mainstream media production, YouTube is a platform for innovation and political activism – a utopian community; for Google and its premium content providers (including CBS, BBC, Universal Music Group, Sony Music Group, Warner Music Group, NBA, The Sundance Channel) and the companies who advertise there, it is a new commercial marketplace. In other words, YouTube is a site for the distribution of both 'top-down' media production from the big corporations and 'bottom-up' grassroots media production. There is also a division between those who see the site as a promotional platform and those who see it as a means for social networking. As Green and Burgess (2009) point out, 'The discomfort of both corporate interests and community participants points to the uncertainty associated with the meaning and uses of YouTube. This uncertainty emerges . . . from its multiple roles as a high-volume website, a broadcast platform, a media archive, and a social network' (5).

If YouTube is an example of participatory culture, the participation of the non-professionals who upload videos and the ordinary people who watch them is fundamental to the commercial success of the site. It is the intensity of the uploading and viewing traffic that YouTube points to in order to encourage advertisers to use the site (see http://www.youtube.com/advertise). Depending on one's involvement, it is a community that is understood as a market and a market that is understood as a community. For some it is simply a video distribution platform, a chance to promote oneself or to advertise a corporate product or service, while for others it is an opportunity to interact with people, to share and respond to the videos that form the fabric of the YouTube community.[8] In a sample of the most popular material on YouTube, Burgess and Green found than user-created content was slightly more popular that industry-generated content (41). But what was most interesting was the content of the Most Responded and Most Discussed categories, where user-created content comprised 63 and 69 per cent respectively, whereas these percentages were reversed in the Most Viewed category (Burgess and Green, 2009: 51-2). What this suggests is that responding and discussing are fundamental to the culture of YouTube. In other words, within the marketplace of YouTube is a community struggling to take shape – struggling over what kind of community it might be. I think Burgess and Green capture well this core tension:

> YouTube needs to be understood as both a business . . . and as a cultural resource co-created by its users . . . The truth is that both of these very different ideas of what YouTube is for are real and co-existing, if not always happily; at various times, as with claims about copyright infringement, the faultlines emerge. (2009: 35)

It is very hard to predict what YouTube will become. Its rapid rise to being a significant media platform should make us wary of making easy predictions. But one thing does seem certain: it will continue to be a site where corporate and grassroots interests exist in an uneasy alliance. And unless we take seriously these two fundamental aspects of YouTube, we will not understand its nature or its development.

> YouTube is a commercial enterprise. But it is also a platform designed to enable cultural participation by ordinary citizens. It is a highly visible example of the broader trend toward uneasy convergences of market and non-market modes of cultural production in the digital environment, where marginal, subcultural, and community-based modes of cultural production are by design incorporated within the commercial logics of major. (2009: 75)

In other words, the culture of YouTube is driven by both commercial and non-commercial forces. It is this entanglement of these forces that makes YouTube difficult to understand using the traditional conceptual tools of media studies. However, it is too soon to tell whether or not YouTube, and sites like it, justify yet the use of the term post-television.

NOTES

1. The essay was first presented as a paper to the Council of Europe Colloquy on 'Training in Critical Reading of Television Language', September 1973, and subsequently published as Centre for

Contemporary Cultural Studies Stencilled Occasional Paper no. 7 in the same year. The diagram (Figure 1) and quotations are from Hall's 1980 revised version (Hall et al. 1980).

2. Patrick Meehan was released from prison in 1977 after serving six years of a life sentence for murder. When interviewed on *Nationwide* he claimed he had been framed by British Intelligence. The interview was marked by a struggle between Meehan's attempt to talk about political issues surrounding his conviction and *Nationwide*'s attempt to 'frame' the interview in terms of personal matters, such as what it was like being in prison. For more details, see Brunsdon and Morley (1978).

3. One interesting problem about the model is the way in which it seems always to assume encoding from a dominant position. What happens to the model when the encoded message is 'radical' or 'progressive'? See Dyer (1977). Another problem is that it assumes we can discover the intention driving a particular encoding. Although clearly influenced by Gramsci's concept of hegemony, the model is still too reliant on ideas of 'dominant ideology'.

4 According to Louis Althusser, 'all ideology has the function (which defines it) of "constructing" concrete individuals as subjects' (2009: 309). Ideological subjects are produced by acts of 'hailing' or 'interpellation'. Althusser uses the analogy of a police officer hailing an individual: 'Hey, you there!' When the individual hailed turns in response, he or she has been interpellated, has become a subject of the police officer's discourse. In this way, ideology is a material practice which creates subjects who are in turn subjected to its specific patterns of thought and modes of behaviour.

5. Since the publication of *The 'Nationwide' Audience*, Morley has sought both to clarify and modify its theoretical and methodological claims. For details see Morley 1980, 1986, 1992. For critical commentaries on the encoding/decoding model, and on Morley's use of it, see Ang 1989, Grossberg 1983, Jancovich 1992, Lewis 1983, Moores 1993, Turner 2003. See Cruz and Lewis 1994 for an interview with Stuart Hall on the encoding/decoding model.

6. Fiske is referring to Liebes and Katz (1993). This work is briefly discussed in Chapter 8.

7. One interesting form of extension might be how in chatrooms or in the virtual worlds of the avatar self, such as Second Life or The Sims, our identities are stretch out anonymously across the network.

8. There is another division in the YouTube community between those who wish to broadcast themselves as part of the ongoing development of a community and those who see an opportunity to broadcast themselves to fortune and fame. Perhaps at times the division between the two is hard to distinguish.

3

FICTION

In *Culture and Environment* (first published in 1933), F. R. Leavis and Denys Thompson (1977) condemn popular fiction for offering addictive forms of 'compensation' and 'distraction'. Moreover, they add, '[t]his form of compensation . . . is the very reverse of recreation, in that it tends, not to strengthen and refresh the addict for living, but to increase his unfitness by habituating him to weak evasions, to the refusal to face reality at all' (100). Q. D. Leavis (1978), in *Fiction and the Reading Public* (first published in 1932), refers to such reading as 'a drug addiction to fiction' (152), adding that for those readers of romantic fiction it can lead to 'a habit of fantasying [which] will lead to maladjustment in actual life' (54). Self-abuse is bad enough, but there is worse: their addiction 'helps to make a social atmosphere unfavourable to the aspirations of the ["cultural"] minority. They actually get in the way of genuine feeling and responsible thinking' (74).

Half a century later, we witness a marked change in attitude. Here is Derek Longhurst (1989), introducing a collection of essays on popular fiction:

> It is now widely recognized that the study of popular fiction plays an important part in cultural analysis. No longer is

reading popular fiction generally considered to be an activity akin to a secret vice to which one should admit shamefacedly. Nor can popular narrative be adequately understood as merely narcotic and its readers as unenlightened junkies. (xi)

Although the distance between the elitist fantasies of the Leavisites and the cultural studies of Longhurst is immense and contains a story worth telling of theoretical and methodological battles won and lost, the rest of this chapter will focus instead on four significant approaches to the study of popular fiction in cultural studies: symptomatic reading, reception theory, reading formations, and feminism and romance reading.

IDEOLOGY AND SYMPTOMATIC READING

According to Louis Althusser (1969), ideological discourse is a closed system. As such, it can only ever set itself such problems as it can answer. To remain secure within its self-imposed boundaries, it must stay silent on questions which threaten to take it beyond these boundaries. This formulation leads Althusser to the concept of the 'problematic'. A problematic is the theoretical (and ideological) structure which both frames and produces the repertoire of crisscrossing and competing discourses out of which a text is materially organised. The problematic of a text relates to its moment of historical existence as much by what it excludes as by what it includes. That is to say, it encourages a text to answer questions posed by itself, but at the same time it generates the production of 'deformed' answers to the question which it attempts to exclude. Thus a problematic is structured as much by what is absent (what is not said) as by what is present (what is said). The task of an Althusserian critical practice is to deconstruct the text (read it symptomatically) to reveal the workings of its problematic and thus establish its relationship to its historical conditions of existence.

Althusser characterises Karl Marx's method of reading the work of Adam Smith as 'symptomatic' in that

it divulges the undivulged event in the text it reads, and in the same movement relates it to a *different text*, present as a

43

necessary absence in the first. Like his first reading, Marx's second reading presupposes the existence of *two texts*, and the measurement of the first against the second. But what distinguishes this new reading from the old is the fact that in the new one the second text is articulated with the lapses in the first text. (1979: 28)

By a symptomatic reading of Smith, Marx is able to measure 'the problematic initially visible in his writings against the invisible problematic contained in the paradox of *an answer which does not correspond to any question posed*' (28). Therefore, to read a text symptomatically is to perform a double reading: reading first the manifest text, and then, through the lapses and distortions, silences and absences (the 'symptoms' of a problem struggling to be posed) in the manifest text, to produce and read the latent text, the problematic.

Undoubtedly the most sustained attempt to apply this method of reading to fictional texts is Pierre Macherey's *A Theory of Literary Production* (1978). Macherey rejects what he calls 'the interpretative fallacy', the view that a text has a single meaning which it is the task of criticism to uncover. For him, the text is not a puzzle which conceals a meaning; it is a construction with a multiplicity of meanings. To 'explain' a text is to recognise this. Moreover, to do so it is necessary to break with the idea that a text is a harmonious unity spiralling forth from an 'original' moment of creation, a moment of supreme intentionality. Against this, he claims that the fictional text is 'decentred'; it is incomplete in itself. To say this does not mean that something needs to be added in order to make it whole. His point is that all fictional texts are 'decentred' (not centred on an authorial intention) in the specific sense that they consist of a confrontation between several discourses: explicit, implicit, silent and absent. The task of critical practice is to explain the disparities in the text which point to a conflict of meanings.

> This conflict is not the sign of an imperfection; it reveals the inscription of an otherness in the work, through which it maintains a relationship with that which it is not, that which happens at its margins. To explain the work is to show that, contrary to appearances, it is not independent, but bears in its

material substance the imprint of a determinate absence which is also the principle of its identity. The book is furrowed by the allusive presence of those other books against which it is elaborated; it circles about the absence of that which it cannot say, haunted by the absence of certain repressed words which make their return. The book is not the extension of a meaning; it is generated from the incompatibility of several meanings, the strongest bond by which it is attached to reality, in a tense and ever-renewed confrontation. (79–80)

Macherey's approach should not be confused with one of literary criticism's traditional tasks – making explicit what is implicit in the text; making audible that which is merely a whisper (i.e. a single meaning). For Macherey, it is not a question of making what is there speak with more clarity so as to be finally sure of the text's meaning. Because a text's meanings are 'both interior and absent', simply to repeat the text's self knowledge is to fail really to explain the text (78). The task of critical practice is not to make a whisper audible, but to produce a new knowledge of the text, one that explains the ideological necessity of its silences, its absences, its structuring incompleteness – the staging of that which it cannot speak.

The act of knowing is not like listening to a discourse already constituted, a mere fiction which we have simply to translate. It is rather the elaboration of a new discourse, the articulation of a silence. Knowledge is not the discovery or reconstruction of a latent meaning, forgotten or concealed. It is something newly raised up, an addition to the reality from which it begins. (6)

Borrowing from Sigmund Freud's (1986) work on dreams, Macherey contends that in order for something to be said, other things must be left unsaid. It is the reason(s) for these absences, these silences, within a text which must be interrogated. 'What is important in the work is what it does not say' (87). Again, like Freud, who believed that the meanings of his patients' problems were not hidden in their conscious discourse but repressed in the turbulent discourse of the unconscious, necessitating a subtle form of analysis acute to the difference between what is said and what is shown, Macherey's approach explores the contradictions between telling and showing. He claims that there is always a 'gap', an 'internal distanciation', between what a text wants to say and what a text actually says. To explain a text, it is necessary to go beyond it, to understand what it 'is compelled to say in order to say what it wants to say' (94). It is here that the text's 'unconscious' (the Althusserian 'problematic') is constituted. And it is in a text's 'unconscious' that its relationship to the ideological and historical conditions of its existence is revealed. It is here, in the absent centre, hollowed out by conflicting discourses, that the text is related to history.

According to Macherey, all narratives contain an ideological project. That is, they promise to tell the 'truth' about something. Information is initially withheld on the promise that it will be revealed. Narrative always constitutes a movement towards disclosure. It begins with a truth promised and ends with a truth revealed. To be rather schematic, Macherey divides the text into two instances: the ideological project (the 'truth' promised), and the realisation (the 'truth' revealed); the 'rupture' between the two (produced by an act of symptomatic reading) reveals the 'unconscious' of the text – the return of the repressed, historical 'truth'.

The text's 'unconscious' does not reflect historical contradictions; rather, it evokes, stages and displays them, allowing us not a 'scientific' knowledge of ideology but an awareness of 'ideology in contradiction with itself' (130); breaking down before questions it cannot answer; failing to do what ideology is supposed to do – 'ideology exists precisely in order to efface all trace of contradiction' (131). 'Science', according to Macherey, destroys ideology; the fictional text challenges ideology by using it, making it visible and therefore available to analysis and contestation. In his discussion, for example, of the work of the French popular science-fiction writer Jules Verne, he shows how Verne's work *stages* the contradictions of late nineteenth-century French imperialism. He contends that the ideological project of Verne's work is the *fantastic* staging of the adventures of French imperialism: its colonising conquest of the earth. Each adventure concerns the hero's conquest of Nature (a mysterious island, the moon, the bottom of the sea, the centre of the earth). In telling these stories, Verne is 'compelled' to tell

46

another: each voyage of conquest becomes a voyage of rediscovery as Verne's heroes discover that others have either been there before or are there already. The significance of this, for Macherey, lies in the disparity which he perceives between 'representation' (what is intended: the subject of the narrative) and 'figuration' (how it is realised: its inscription in narrative): Verne 'represents' the ideology of French imperialism, while at the same time, through the act of 'figuration' (making material in the *form* of a fiction), undermines one of its central myths in the continual staging of the fact that the lands are always already occupied. 'In the passage from the level of representation to that of figuration, ideology undergoes a complete *modification* . . . perhaps because no ideology is sufficiently consistent to survive the test of figuration' (194–5). Thus, by giving fictional form to the ideology of imperialism, Verne's work – 'to read it against the grain of its intended meaning' (230) – stages the contradictions between the myth and the reality of imperialism. The stories do not provide us with a 'scientific' denunciation ('a knowledge in the strict sense') of imperialism, but by an act of symptomatic reading, 'which dislodges the work internally' (161), they 'make us see', 'make us perceive', 'make us feel' the terrible contradictions of the ideological discourses from which each text of Verne's is constituted: 'from which it is born, in which it bathes, from which it detaches itself . . . and to which it alludes' (Althusser 1971: 222). Verne's science-fantasy adventure stories show us – though not in the way(s) intended – the ideological and historical conditions of their existence.

RECEPTION THEORY

In his major work, *Truth and Method*, Hans-Georg Gadamer argues that an understanding of a cultural text is always from the perspective of the person who understands. Authors may have intentions, and texts certainly have material structures, but meaning is not something inherent in a text (an unchanging essence); meaning is always something a person makes when he or she reads a text. Moreover, Gadamer is adamant that texts and readers always encounter each other in historical and social locations and that the situatedness of this encounter always informs the interaction between reader and text. In this way, he contends, a text is always read with preconceptions or prejudices; it is never encountered in a state of virginal purity, untouched by the knowledge with which, or the context in which, it is read. This is not, for Gadamer, something to regret, in a vain appeal to 'the ontological obstructions of the scientific concept of objectivity' (235), rather these are the necessary conditions for understanding. It is through our preconceptions and prejudices that we organise our approach to a text. As Gadamer explains, 'the historicity of our existence entails that prejudices, in the literal sense of the word [pre-judgements], constitute the initial directedness of our whole ability to experience' (9). We always begin the task of understanding with 'our own fore-meanings ... [our] own expectations of meaning' (238).

This does not mean that our understanding of a text (its meaning)[1] is therefore a subjective event, leading to the suggestion that any meaning can be subjectively imposed upon a text. Preconceptions or prejudices, as Gadamer insists, are not the same as 'false judgments' (240). Furthermore, although we approach a text with precon-ceived ideas, what we always encounter is the materiality of the text itself (particular words ordered in particular ways, which allow the reader to recognise a difference between, say, Shakespeare's Sonnet 138 and 'Sailing to Byzantium' by W. B. Yeats). This is of course an encounter in which our preconceived ideas may well be modified. An understanding of a text (its meaning) is therefore always a proc-ess in which preconceived ideas are confronted (and perhaps modi-fied) by the materiality of the text. He describes this process, what he calls the 'hermeneutic circle' (259), as working like a dialogue of questions and answers: we ask questions of a text, but if a satisfac-tory understanding is to be achieved we must always remain open to the answers it gives to the questions we ask. Both text and reader bring something to the encounter. In this way, 'meanings cannot be understood in an arbitrary way ... we cannot hold blindly to our own fore-meaning ... we [must] remain open to the meaning ... of the text. But this openness always includes our placing the other meaning [the meaning of the text] in a relation with the whole of our own meanings' (238).

48

However, as Gadamer insists, 'Not occasionally only, but always, the meaning of a text goes beyond its author. That is why understanding is not merely . . . reproductive [simply activating the 'meaning' in the text], but [is] always . . . productive [producing a 'meaning' in the interaction between text and reader]' (264). He describes this process of dialogue between reader and text in which meaning is made as a 'fusion of horizons' (273). The 'horizon of understanding' (conceptual framework; the taken for granted) of the reader confronts the 'horizon of understanding' of the text. It is in the space opened up between the two that meaning is made in a 'fusion of horizons of understanding' (340). In this way, understanding is a process of 're-creation', which is 'both bound and free' (107). As he explains, 'the discovery of the true meaning of a text or a work of art is never finished; it is in fact an infinite process. Not only are fresh sources of error constantly excluded, so that the true meaning has filtered out of it all kinds of things that obscure it, but there emerge continually new sources of understanding, which reveal unsuspected elements of meaning' (266). In other words, both text and reader are always historically situated, and therefore the encounter between the two is always a fusion of different historical horizons.

Wolfgang Iser is a German literary theorist, a member of the Constance School of reception theory. Like Gadamer, Iser insists that the act of reading is always an act of production. He maintains that 'As a literary text can only produce a response when it is read, it is virtually impossible to describe this response without also analysing the reading process . . . the text represents a potential effect that is realized in the reading process . . . the meaning of the text is something that [the reader] has to assemble' (1978: ix). The production of meaning, therefore, involves 'a dialectic relationship between text, reader, and their interaction' (x). Moreover, as Iser insists, 'meaning is [not] an object to be defined, but is an effect to be experienced' (10). It follows from this that the real focus of a literary critic should not be 'to teach the reader the meaning of the text, for without a subjective contribution and a context there is no such thing' (19). Rather, the object of study should be 'an analysis of what actually happens when one is reading a text, for that is when the text begins to unfold its potential; it is in the reader that the text comes to life' (ibid.). As he explains:

> Central to the reading of every literary work is the interaction between its structure and its recipient. [Therefore] . . . the study of a literary work should concern not only the actual text itself but also, and in equal measure, the actions involved in responding to that text. The text itself simply offers 'schematised aspects' through which the subject matter of the work can be produced, while the actual production takes place through an act of concretization. (20–1)

Iser distinguishes between the text, the work, and the reader. As he explains:

> The literary work has two poles, which we might call the artistic and the aesthetic: the artistic pole is the author's text and the aesthetic is the realization accomplished by the reader. In view of this polarity, it is clear that the work itself cannot be identical with the text or with the concretization, but must be situated somewhere between the two. (21)

As he contends, 'the meaning of a literary text is not a definable entity but, if anything, a dynamic happening' (22). The text in effect, he argues, offers itself for 'performance' by a reader. In this way, 'literary texts initiate "performances" of meaning rather than actually formulating meanings themselves . . . [and, moreover] without the participation of the individual reader there can be no performance' (27).

In other words, although the text is produced by the author, it is the reader, according to Iser, who brings the text to life, and thus brings the work into existence. Therefore, it is in the act of reading that meaning is realised. However, although the text, in its potential as a performance script, offers to the reader 'certain conditions of actualisation' (34), or what he called in an earlier argument, a range of 'polysemantic possibilities' (1974: 136), it still presents itself to the reader as a material structure, 'the repertoire of the text' (1978: 69), and thus limits the play of interpretation. There is always, therefore, 'the role offered by the text and the reader's own disposition, and as one can never be fully taken over by the other, there arises between the two [a] tension' (37).

Although in general terms, 'the role prescribed by the text will be the stronger . . . the reader's own disposition will never disappear totally' (ibid.). Performance of meaning always takes place in a context; the nature of the context both 'illuminates and stabilises the meaning' (62). Iser figures the literary text as an instruction manual for the performance of meaning. The repertoire of the text 'forms an organizational structure of meaning which must be optimised through the reading of the text. This optimisation will depend on the reader's own degree of awareness and on his willingness to open himself up to an unfamiliar experience' (85). However, the repertoire of the text cannot totally determine the performance of meaning: the repertoire of the text 'can only offer the reader *possibilities* of organization. Total organization would mean that there was nothing left for the reader to do' (86). Moreover, 'the reader's task is not simply to accept, but to assemble for himself that which is to be accepted' (97). As he observes:

> Although the reader must participate in the assembly of meaning by realizing the structure inherent in the text, it must not be forgotten that he stands outside the text. His position must therefore be manipulated by the text if his viewpoint is to be properly guided. Clearly, this viewpoint cannot be determined exclusively by the individual reader's personal history of experience, but this history cannot be totally ignored either: only when the reader has been taken outside his own experience can his viewpoint be changed. The constitution of meaning, therefore, gains its full significance when something happens to the reader. The constituting of meaning and the constituting of the reading subject are therefore interacting operations that are both structured by the aspects of the text. (152)

As Iser contends, 'Reading is an activity that is guided by the text; this must be processed by the reader, who is then, in turn, affected by what he has processed' (163). In this way, reading can be seen as a creative process in which the text 'offers guidance as to what is to be produced, and therefore cannot itself be the product' (107). The difference he draws our attention to, between a text offering guidance on how it should be read, and the text as the end product of reading, is an important theoretical distinction. It is a challenge to the many theoretical perspectives which advocate a view of meaning as something imposed on a reader by a text. As Iser maintains, 'Reading is not a direct "internalisation", because it is not a one-way process . . . [it is] a dynamic *interaction* between text and reader' (ibid.).

Hans Robert Jauss, a former student of Gadamer's, is a literary historian and, like Iser, is a member of the Constance School. Although he shares Iser's view that the indeterminacy of the text requires a reader to realise its meaning, he also insists, against Iser's rather asocial/ahistorical reader, that readers and readings are always historically situated within specific conditions of reading. This is a rejection of the widespread 'belief in the timeless substance of a literary work and in the timeless point of view of the reader' (1982: 196). As he maintains:

> A literary work is not an object which stands by itself and that offers the same view to each reader in each period. It is not a monument that monologically reveals its timeless essence. It is much more like an orchestration that strikes ever new resonances among its readers and frees the text from the material of the words and brings it to a contemporary existence. (21)

Therefore, if we are to understand fully the process of reading, he argues, readers and their readings must be located in specific historical conditions of reading. The reading of a text is always mediated by what Jauss calls a 'horizon of expectations' (22).

> A literary work, even when it appears to be new, does not present itself as something absolutely new in an informational vacuum, but predisposes its audience to a very specific kind of reception by announcements, overt and covert signals, familiar characteristics, or implicit allusions. It awakens memories of that which was already read, brings the reader to a specific emotional attitude, and with its beginning arouses

expectations for the 'middle and end', which can then be maintained intact or altered, reoriented, or even fulfilled ironically in the course of the reading according to specific rules of the genre or type of text. (23)

In other words, texts are always read in the knowledge of other texts already read; information already stored, and available for use, in the cultural storehouse of the reader.

So far the theories we have considered are all predicated on the notion that literary texts place clear limits on their possible interpretation. Iser, for example, describes his work as a theory of 'aesthetic response' and not a theory of 'aesthetic reception' (1978: x). The distinction he is concerned to make is between an approach which begins with the text and one which starts with the reader. 'A theory of reception . . . always deals with existing readers, whose reactions testify to certain historically conditioned experiences of literature. A theory of response has its roots in the text; a theory of reception arises from a history of readers' judgments' (ibid.). The next example to be discussed is the work of the American literary critic Stanley Fish. As we shall see, he very definitely begins with the reader.

Literature, as Stanley Fish contends, 'is an open category, not definable by fictionality, or by a disregard of propositional truth, or by a prominence of tropes and figures, but simply by what we decide to put into it' (1980: 11). This does not mean that what counts as literature is determined by the subjective will of individual readers; the 'we' Fish refers to is the 'literary community'. As he explains, 'the act of recognising literature is not constrained by something in the text, nor does it issue from an independent and arbitrary will; rather, it proceeds from a collective decision that will be in force only so long as a community of readers or believers continues to abide by it' (ibid.). It follows from this, Fish contends, that 'there is no single way of reading that is correct or natural, only "ways of seeing" that are extensions of . . . [the] perspectives [of] interpretative communities' (16). The literary community is thus divided into different interpretative communities, each with its own set of interests and concerns, and each seeking to win support for its own particular 'set of interpretative assumptions' (ibid.). Moreover, Fish insists that 'interpretation is the source of texts, facts, authors, and intentions'; all are 'the *products* of interpretation' (16–17).

Interpretative communities provide specific contexts for operating as a reader. In this way, the meaning of a text is always a situated meaning, produced in a specific context. As he contends, 'meanings are the property neither of fixed and stable texts nor of free and independent readers but of interpretative communities that are responsible both for the shape of a reader's activities and for the texts those activities produce' (322). Moreover, it is not possible for a text to have a meaning outside a specific situation. As Fish explains:

> communication occurs within situations and that to be in a situation is already to be in possession of (or to be possessed by) a structure of assumptions, of practices understood to be relevant in relation to purposes and goals that are already in place; and it is within the assumption of these purposes and goals that any utterance is *immediately* heard. (318)[2]

Fish offers the example of what a group of poetry students were able to do with the names of four linguists and one literary critic, left on the blackboard from a previous class. When the poetry students entered the room, he told them that what they saw on the blackboard was a seventeenth-century English religious poem. Armed with this information, the poetry students proceeded to read, in a detailed and convincing manner, the five names on the blackboard as a seventeenth-century English religious poem. What allowed them to do this, according to Fish, is the fact that:

> [i]t is not that the presence of poetic qualities compels a certain kind of attention [the 'common sense' of literary criticism] but that the paying of a certain kind of attention results in the emergence of poetic qualities. As soon as my students were aware that it was poetry they were seeing, they began to look with poetry-seeing eyes, that is, with eyes that saw everything in relation to the properties they knew poems to possess . . . Thus the meanings of the words and the interpretation in which those

words were seen to be embedded emerged together, as a consequence of the operations my students began to perform once
they were told that this was a poem. (326)

This leads Fish to the conclusion that it is not the properties of a
text but the interpretative assumptions and strategies performed by
readers, situated in interpretative communities, which determine the
outcomes of interpretation. In this way, he argues, 'Interpretation is
not the art of construing but the art of constructing. Interpreters do
not decode poems; they make them' (327).

The interpretative strategies of interpretative communities are
always 'social and conventional' (331), therefore, as Fish explains:

> [W]hile it is true to say that we create poetry . . . we create it
> through interpretative strategies that are finally not our own
> but have their source in a publicly available system of intel-
> ligibility. Insofar as the . . . literary system . . . constrains us, it
> also fashions us, furnishing us with categories of understand-
> ing, with which we in turn fashion the entities to which we
> can then point. (332)[3]

READING FORMATIONS

The general focus of Tony Bennett's and Janet Woollacott's
(1987) *Bond and Beyond* is the diverse and changing ways in
which the figure of James Bond has been produced and reproduced through a range of different cultural texts and practices.
Analysis ranges from the novels and films to academic criticism,
showbiz journalism, fanzine articles, advertising copy and interviews with stars and film-makers, to chart the different ways
in which 'the figure of Bond has been put into circulation as a
popular hero' (1).

Bennett and Woollacott reject the view that the texts of popular fiction are little more than containers of ideology, a convenient
and always successful means to transmit dominant ideology from
the culture industries to the duped and manipulated masses. One
of the problems with such a view is that it leads to 'a politics of
simple opposition and to a criticism which is little more than a

constant unmasking of dominant ideologies at work' (4). Against this, they contend that popular fiction is a specific space, with its own ideological economy, making available a historically variable, complex and contradictory range of ideological discourses and counter-discourses to be activated in particular conditions of reading. While they accept that it may be possible to describe the Bond novels and films as racist, sexist and reactionary, to stop there is to fail to explore how these texts engage with a popular audience. That is, of course, '[u]nless one subscribes to the view that the reading, cinema-going and television publics simply enjoy sexist, racist and reactionary texts' (4). Rather than simply condemn these texts, Bennett and Woollacott seek to explore why and how they make their appeal.

James Bond is undoubtedly fiction's most famous spy. The popularity of Bond (certainly during the 1950s, 1960s, 1970s and now again in the twenty-first century) is beyond question. By 1977, the worldwide audience for Bond films was in excess of 1,000 million, while paperback sales in Britain alone totalled 27,863,500. It is Bennett and Woollacott's contention that Bond's popularity resulted from his ability to articulate – to connect and to express – a series of cultural and political concerns. These include the historically mobile ideological relations between West and East, capitalism and communism, masculine and feminine, as well as changing notions of Britishness.

> However, the precise way in which the figure of Bond has articulated . . . these concerns has varied during different moments of his career as a popular hero. The ideological and cultural elements out of which the figure of Bond has been woven may have been constant, but these have been combined in different mixes and shifting permutations. If Bond has functioned as a 'sign of the times', it has been as a *moving sign of the times*, as a figure capable of taking up and articulating quite different and even contradictory cultural and ideological values, sometimes turning its back on the meanings and cultural possibilities it had earlier embodied to enunciate new ones. (19)

Moreover, it is the ideological 'malleability' of the figure of Bond which has ensured his continuing popularity. As Bennett and Woollacott point out, 'it is not the popularity of *Bond* that has to be accounted for so much as the popularity of *different Bonds*, popular in different ways and for different reasons at different points in time' (20). What has remained constant is the way in which Bond 'has functioned as a shifting focal point for the articulation of historically specific ideological concerns' (20).

Bond's first moment of popularity occurs in the late 1950s. The key events are the paperback publication of *Casino Royale* and *Moonraker*, and the serialisation of *From Russia, With Love* in the *Daily Express*, followed by a daily strip-cartoon of Bond in the same newspaper. Sales of the novels in Britain rose from 58,000 in 1956 to 237,000 in 1959. During this period, Bond served as a political hero of the lower middle class.

> Bond . . . functioned first and foremost, although not exclusively, as a Cold War hero, an exemplary representative of the virtues of Western capitalism triumphing over the evils of Eastern communism . . . Bond effects an ideologically loaded imaginary resolution of the real historical contradictions of the period, a resolution in which all the values associated with Bond and, thereby, the West – notably, freedom and individualism – gain ascendancy over those associated with the villain and, thereby, communist Russia, such as totalitarianism and bureaucratic rigidity. (25)

In addition, given that this is the period following the blow to national dignity represented by the fiasco of Suez (1956), it is not surprising that the figure of Bond also articulates an appeal to a more mythic notion of British nationhood. As above all an *British* hero, in a period of marked national decline, Bond seemed to offer the promise of a turning-back of history and a return to a time of world leadership. What could no longer be achieved in the real world might be symbolically brought into play in the fictional world of James Bond.

Bond's second moment occurs in the early 1960s, with the release of the first Bond film, *Dr No*. The effect was twofold. First, it broadened the social base of Bond's popularity. Second, it entailed the 'ideological remodelling' (30) of the figure of Bond. As Bennett and Woollacott explain:

> The various ideological and cultural elements out of which the figure of Bond had earlier been constructed were, so to speak, dismantled and separated from one another in order to be reassembled in a new configuration which pointed, ideologically and culturally, in a number of new and different directions. (30)

The release of the first cycle of Bond films (*Dr No*, 1962; *From Russia, With Love*, 1963; *Goldfinger*, 1964; *Thunderball*, 1965; *You Only Live Twice*, 1967) increased the sales of the novels. It also brought the figure of Bond into the world of advertising and commodity production. But more than this, it modified Bond's ideological and cultural significance. First, it relocated Bond in terms of East–West relations, moving him from Cold War hero to defender of détente. In narrative terms, this meant the replacement of SMERSH by SPECTRE. The enemy was no longer the communist East but an international criminal conspiracy, determined to exploit the still fragile relations between capitalist West and communist East. Second, Bond's Britishshness no longer represented an attempt to put history in reverse, but increasingly became a symbol of the nation running in advance of history – the embodiment of the values of 'swinging Britain'.

> Bond provided a mythic encapsulation of the then prominent ideological themes of classlessness and modernity, a key cultural marker of the claim that Britain had escaped the blinkered, class-bound perspectives of its traditional ruling elites and was in the process of being thoroughly modernised as a result of the implementation of a new, meritocratic style of cultural and political leadership, middle-class and professional rather than aristocratic and amateur. (34–5)

Whereas, in the first moment, Bond's individualism was set in opposition to the mundane bureaucracy of the communist countries of the East, his individualism now signalled the meritocratic culture of a 'classless' Britain, 'swinging' free of the dead weight of the past and 'the allegedly morally sapping effects of welfare socialism' (237). Thus the figure of Bond moved from being a hero of tradition to become a hero of progress, from the past to the promise of the future, as the first cycle of films adjusted the 'inter-textual' (see below) relations in which Bond figured as a popular hero.

A further modification to Bond's ideological currency during this period was the bringing into play, together with the new figure of 'the Bond girl', a new construction of gender and sexual relations.

> Between them, Bond and 'the Bond girl' embodied a modernisation of sexuality, representatives of norms of masculinity and femininity that were 'swinging free' from the constraints of the past. If Bond thus embodied a male sexuality that was freed from the constraints and hypocrisy of gentlemanly chivalry, a point of departure from the restraint, a-sexuality or repressed sexuality of the traditional English aristocratic hero, 'the Bond girl' – tailored to suit Bond's needs – was likewise represented as the subject of a free and independent sexuality, liberated from the constraints of family, marriage and domesticity. The image of 'the Bond girl' thus constituted a model of adjustment, a condensation of the attributes of femininity appropriate to the requirements of the new norms of male sexuality represented by Bond. (35)

The third moment of Bond's career as a popular hero, from the 1970s onwards, is marked by a selective and strategic activation of Bond's already established ideological currency. Bond's popularity is now institutionalised as family entertainment. Still a figure in advertising and commodity production, he is no longer marketed in terms of sexuality or nationhood but through the technology increasingly highlighted in the Bond films – spin-off items aimed at children. There is also a significant contraction in terms of Bond's ideological range. The political concerns of East–West relations and the articulation of Brithishness remain, but mostly to be mocked and parodied. The central ideological focus is now gender and sexuality.

The most significant change associated with the films of this period ... consisted in a shift in the centre of narrative interest, increasingly pronounced as the 1970s progressed, away from the relations between Bond and the villain towards the relations between Bond and 'the Bond girl'. Usually portrayed as 'excessively' independent – a fellow professional who works alongside Bond, threatening to best him in the traditionally masculine preserve of espionage work ... the destiny of 'the Bond girl' in the films of this period is to meet her come-uppance in her encounter with Bond. The main ideological work thus accomplished in the unfolding of the narrative is that of a 'putting-back-in-place' of women who carry their independence and liberation 'too far' or into 'inappropriate' fields of activity. (39)

This is not a new concern (it's there in the novels and the early films). However, what is new is the dominant place which this concern now occupies in the narrative structure, subordinating all other concerns. This change in narrative focus 'clearly constituted a response – in truth, somewhat nervous and uncertain – to the Women's Liberation movement, fictitiously rolling back the advances of feminism to restore an imaginarily more secure phallocentric conception of gender relations' (39).

The point of discussing the films is not simply to draw attention to how they produced a popular readership for the novels. What is of crucial theoretical and methodological interest are the ways in which the films (and other 'texts of Bond') helped to organise and predispose 'readers to read the novels in certain ways, privileging some of their aspects at the expense of others' (43). At the centre of Bennett's and Woollacott's argument is the claim that 'the condition of Bond's existence have been *inter-textual*' (44). They use the hyphen to indicate the theoretical difference between their usage of the term and the way in which the term is usually employed (without the hyphen) within cultural studies to signify the way in which one text is marked by the signs of other texts. As Bennett and Woollacott make clear, their employment of the term is quite different: 'We intend the concept inter-textuality to refer to the social organisation of the relations between texts within specific conditions of reading' (45). Moreover, they argue that 'the latter overrides and overdetermines the former. *Intertextualities* . . . are the product of specific, socially organised *inter-textualities*; it is the latter which, in providing the objective determinants of reading practices, provide the framework within which inter-textual references can be produced and operate' (86). Thus, they argue:

> The figure of Bond has been produced in the constantly changing relations between the wide range of texts brought into association with one another via the functioning of Bond as the signifier which they have jointly constructed. In turn, it is this figure which, in floating between them, has thereby connected these texts into a related set in spite of their manifold differences in other respects. (45)

In other words, what unites these texts is not an author (even the novels are written by a number of authors), but the figure of Bond. It is Bond who 'furnishes the operative principle of textual classification' (52). Moreover, when Bond changes, 'such changes form a part of the social and cultural determination which influence the way the texts concerned are available to be read' (52–3). An objection to this argument might be to claim that the novels (as the original source of Bond) have a privileged status over the other 'texts of Bond'. Bennett and Woollacott claim that such an argument 'is impossible to maintain' (53).

> The 'texts of Bond' have comprised a constantly accumulating and 'mutating' set of texts, 'mutating' in the sense that additions to the set have connected with the pre-existing 'texts of Bond' in such a way as to reorganise kaleidoscopically the relationships, transactions and exchanges between them. None of the texts in which the figure of Bond has been constructed can thus be regarded as privileged in relation to the others in any absolute or permanent sense. Rather, each region of this textual set occupies a privileged position in relation to the others, but in different ways depending on the part it has played in the circulation and expanded reproduction of the figure of Bond. (54)

Therefore, although Fleming's novels came first and supplied much of the material for the subsequent films, once the films were in circulation it was these that dominated constructions of the figure of Bond. As noted earlier, it was the films which produced the popular audience for the novels. But more than this, Bennett and Woollacott would insist, it was the films which provided the interpretative framework through which to read the novels. Once this is acknowledged, the rather one-way relationship (questions of difference and similarity, etc.) usually brought into play in discussions of film adaptations of novels begins to look unconvincing. As Bennett and Woollacott contend, the films 'have culturally activated the novels in particular ways, selectively cueing their reading, modifying the exchange between text and reader, inflecting it in new directions by inserting the novels within an expanded inter-textual set' (55).

The point can be illustrated by considering how different Bond might appear to a reader who reads the novels (pre-film adaptations) as belonging to the tradition of the imperialist spy-thriller as against the reader who reads them having seen the first cycle of Bond films.[4] Neither would produce the 'true' response; no more so than, say, the American readers who located the novels in the tradition of hard-boiled fiction or the romance readers who read Bond as a classic romantic hero. What these possible readings point to is the way in which reading is always:

> profoundly affected by the reader's specific preorientation to the novels produced by his or her insertion in the orders of inter-textuality which, in different ways for different groups of readers in different circumstances, hover between text and reader, connecting the two within specific horizons of intelligibility. The process of reading is not one in which reader and text meet as abstractions but one in which the inter-textually organised reader meets the inter-textually organised text. The exchange is never a pure one between two unsullied entities, existing separately from one another, but is rather 'muddied' by the cultural debris which attach to both texts and readers in the determinate conditions which regulate the specific forms of their encounter . . . The Bond novels now reach us

already humming with the meanings established by the films and, as a consequence, have been hooked into orders of inter-textuality to which, initially, they were not connected. (56)

Bennett and Woollacott reject both the view that the text deter-mines its own reading (invites recognition of its objective proper-ties) and the apparently contrary view that it is the reader who produces the meaning of the text. They accuse both approaches of working with a 'metaphysical view of texts' (60), in that the first claims that the meaning of a text pre-exists its conditions of read-ing, while the second, although accepting the possibility of variable readings, nonetheless insists that these are variable readings of the *same* text. Against both of these positions, they argue for a rethink-ing of the text–reader relationship.

> This entails that these texts [the Bond novels] be conceived as having no existence prior to or independently of the vary-ing 'reading formations' in which they have been constituted as objects-to-be-read. By 'reading formations' here, we have in mind not the generalised cultural determinations of read-ing considered by David Morley [see Chapter 2 above], but those specific determinations which bear in upon, mould and configure the relations between texts and readers in deter-minant conditions of reading. It [reading formations] refers, specifically, to the inter-textual relations which prevail in a particular context, thereby activating a given body of texts by ordering the relations between them in a specific way such that their reading is always-already cued in specific directions that are not given by those 'texts themselves' as entities sepa-rable from such relations. (64)

Bennett and Woollacott claim that both texts and readers are 'always-already culturally activated' (64) to the extent that the distinction between subject and object is continually blurred. As they contend, 'Text and reader are conceived as being co-produced within a reading formation, gridded on to one another in a deter-minate compact unity' (64). In other words, a text only becomes a text when read, just as a reader only becomes a reader in the act of reading; neither can exist outside this relationship. This of course exposes Bennett and Woollacott to the accusation that they are claiming that readers and texts have no objective existence. They clarify as follows:

> This is not to suggest that texts have no determinate properties – such as a definite order of narrative progression – which may be analysed objectively. But it is to argue that such properties cannot, in themselves, validate certain received meanings above others; they do not provide a point of 'truth' in relation to which readings may be normatively and hierarchically ranked, or discounted. Nor are we suggesting that readers do not have determinate properties. They most certainly do, but complexly varying ones which, rather than being attributable to the reader as a subject independent of the text, are the product of the orders of inter-textuality which have marked the reader's formation. (65)

Bennett and Woollacott's purpose, therefore, in detailing the different moments in the construction of Bond as a popular hero is not to make claims about the 'true' meaning of Bond. 'On the contrary,' as they explain, 'we have contended that neither the meanings nor the meaning-producing structures of texts can be specified independently of the reading formations which regulate reading practices' (141–2). Regimes of inter-textuality organise how readers read texts. We never get access to texts 'in themselves', but always as situated within a network of inter-textual relations.

> We have thus, in approaching the various individual 'texts of Bond', stressed the degree to which these have always been variably produced – not as 'the same text' but as different 'texts-to-be-read' – as a result of their insertion within different regimes of inter-textuality. Further, we have suggested that it is not possible to abstract any of the individual texts of Bond from the mobile and changing systems of inter-textual relationships through which their reading has been organised in order to constitute a space in which such texts might be stabilised as possible objects of knowledge 'in themselves'. (260–1)

In other words, text and context are not separate moments available for analysis at different times. Text and context are always part of the same process, the same moment – they are inseparable: one cannot have a text without a context, or context without a text. Moreover, Bennett and Woollacott contend that all previous approaches to the question of meaning-production have assumed that one can separate textual meaning from the meanings produced in actual acts of reading. The first supposedly approximates to the essential properties of the text (and can be determined without reference to factors outside or beyond the text); the second, influenced (muddled and blurred) by extra-textual variables, may change through history and across cultures, but it is still a reading of (a variation on) the essential properties of the text (in other words, different readings of the same text). This is a mode of analysis, which, despite its reference to the activities of readers, always ends up privileging the text. There is an objective structure and there is the endless flow of subjective responses. Drawing on the work of the French linguist Michel Pêcheux (1982), Bennett and Woollacott argue that meaning (or reading) does not exist prior to its articulation by a reader. It cannot pre-exist the encounter between reader and text. This is not an attempt to reduce text to context, but an insistence that context and text cannot be conceived of as separate entities. 'The concept of reading formation . . . is an attempt to think of contexts of reception as sets of discursive and inter-textual determinations which, in operating on both texts and readers, mediate the relations between them and provide the mechanisms through which they can productively interact' (263).[5] They do not deny that texts have a material existence. But they do insist that the most adequate way to conceive of a text is 'as a historically constituted object rather than as a metaphysical essence' (266).

Similarly, they also insist that we must distinguish between the subject positions offered by texts and the 'social subject' who may or may not take up the invitation offered. In addition, they contend that the subject positions offered by texts 'only exist in relation to regimes of inter-textuality, within which "social subjects" exist and from which they read texts' (229). Subjects are not constructed by texts, but by regimes of inter-textuality.

Much previous debate on the question of reading has dead-locked on the opposition between the view of the text as dictating its readings and the view that readers are able to mobilise cultural resources which enable them to read against the grain of the text or to negotiate its meanings in particular ways. Our purpose has been to displace the terms of this dispute by suggesting that neither approach takes sufficient account of the cultural and ideological forces which organise and reorganise the network of inter-textual relations within which texts are inserted as texts-to-be-read in certain ways by reading subjects organised to read in certain ways. The relations between texts and readers, we have suggested, are always profoundly mediated by the discursive and inter-textual determinations which, operating on both, structure the domain of their encounter so as to produce, always in specific and variable forms, texts and readers as the mutual supports of one another. (249)

FEMINISM AND ROMANCE READING

In *Loving with a Vengeance*, Tania Modleski (1982) claims that women writing about 'feminine narratives' tend to adopt one of three possible positions: 'dismissiveness; hostility – tending unfortunately to be aimed at the consumers of the narratives; or, most frequently, a flippant kind of mockery' (14). Against this, she declares: '[i]t is time to begin a feminist reading of women's reading' (34). She argues that these popular narratives 'speak to very real problems and tensions in women's lives' (14). Despite this, she acknowledges that the way in which these narratives resolve problems and tensions will rarely 'please modern feminists: far from it' (25). However, the reader of fantasies and the feminist reader do have something in common: dissatisfaction with women's lives.

Rosalind Coward's (1984) interest in romantic fiction is in part inspired by the claim that '[o]ver the past decade, the rise of feminism has been paralleled almost exactly by a mushroom growth in the popularity of romantic fiction' (190). Coward believes two things about romantic fiction: that 'they must still satisfy some very definite needs', and that they offer evidence of, and contribute to, 'a very powerful and common fantasy' (190). She claims that the fantasies played out in romantic fiction are 'pre-adolescent, very nearly pre-conscious' (191–2). She believes them to be 'regressive' in two key respects. On the one hand, they adore the power of the male in ways reminiscent of the very early child-father relationship, while on the other, they are regressive because of the attitude taken to female sexual desire – passive and without guilt, as the responsibility for sexual desire is projected on the male; sexual desire is something that men have and to which women merely respond. In short, romantic fiction replays the girl's experience of the Oedipal drama, only this time without its conclusion in female powerlessness; this time she does marry the father and replace the mother. Therefore there is a trajectory from subordination to position of power (as the mother figure). But, as Coward points out:

> [r]omantic fiction is surely popular because it . . . restores the childhood world of sexual relations and suppresses criticisms of the inadequacy of men, the suffocation of the family, or the damage inflicted by patriarchal power. Yet it simultaneously manages to avoid the guilt and fear which might come from that childhood world. Sexuality is defined firmly as the father's responsibility, and fear of suffocation is overcome because women achieve a sort of power in romantic fiction. Romantic fiction promises a secure world, promises that there will be safety with dependence, that there will be power with subordination. (196)

Janice Radway's *Reading the Romance* (1987) has been described by Charlotte Brunsdon (1991) as 'the most extensive scholarly investigation of the act of reading', crediting Radway with having installed in the classroom '[t]he figure of the ordinary woman' (372). Radway's study is based on research she carried out in 'Smithton', involving a group of forty-two romance readers (mostly married with children). Her research was conducted through individual questionnaires, open-ended group discussions, face-to-face interviews, some informal discussions, and by observing the interactions between the different members of Smithton's symbolic community of romance readers.

According to the Smithton women, the ideal romance is one in which an intelligent and independent woman with a good sense of humour is overwhelmed, after much suspicion and distrust, and some cruelty and violence, by the love of an intelligent, tender and good-humoured man, who in the course of their relationship is transformed from an emotional preliterate to someone who can *care* for her and *nurture* her in ways that traditionally we would expect only from a woman to a man. As Radway explains: '[t]he romantic fantasy is . . . not a fantasy about discovering a uniquely interesting life partner, but a ritual wish to be cared for, loved, and validated in a particular way' (83). It is a fantasy about reciprocation; the wish to believe that men can bestow on women the care and attention that women are expected regularly to bestow on men. But the romantic fantasy offers more than this; it recalls a time when the reader was in fact the recipient of an intense 'maternal' care. Drawing on the work of Nancy Chodorow (1978), Radway claims that romantic fantasy is a form of regression in which the reader is imaginatively and emotionally transported to a time 'when she was the center of a profoundly nurturant individual's attention' (84). Romance reading, Radway argues, is a fantasy in which the hero is eventually the source of care and attention not experienced by the reader since she was a pre-Oedipal child. In this way, romance reading can be viewed as a means by which women can vicariously, through the hero–heroine relationship, experience the emotional succour which they themselves are expected to provide to others without adequate reciprocation for themselves in their normal day-to-day existence.

Radway also takes from Chodorow the notion of the female self as a self-in-relation to others, and the male self as a self autonomous and independent. Chodorow argues that this results from the different relations that a girl and boy have with their mother. Radway sees a correlation between the psychological events described by Chodorow and the narrative pattern of the ideal romance: in the journey from identity in crisis to identity restored, 'the heroine successfully establishes by the end of the ideal narrative . . . the now-familiar female self, the self-in-relation' (134). Radway also takes from Chodorow the belief that women emerge from the Oedipal complex with a 'triangular psychic structure intact'. The result is that 'not only do they need to connect themselves with a member of the opposite sex, but they also continue to require an intense emotional bond with someone who is reciprocally nurturant and protective in a maternal way' (140). In order to experience this regression to maternal emotional fulfilment, she has three options: lesbianism, a relationship with a man, or to seek fulfilment by other means. The homophobic nature of our culture limits the first; the nature of masculinity limits the second; romance reading may be an example of the third. Radway contends that:

> the fantasy that generates the romance originates in the oedipal desire to love and be loved by an individual of the opposite sex *and* in the continuing pre-oedipal wish that is part of a woman's inner-object configuration, the wish to regain the love of the mother and all that it implies – erotic pleasure, symbiotic completion, and identity confirmation. (146)

The resolution to the ideal romance provides perfect triangular satisfaction: 'fatherly protection, motherly care, and passionate adult love' (149).

The failed romance is unable to provide these satisfactions because on the one hand it is too violent, and on the other it concludes sadly, or with an unconvincing happy ending. This highlights in an unpleasurable way the two structuring anxieties of all romances. The first is the fear of male violence. In the ideal romance, this is contained by revealing it to be not the fearful thing it appears to be; it is either an illusion or 'benign'. The second anxiety is the 'fear of an awakened female sexuality and its impact on men' (169). In the failed romance, female sexuality is not confined to a permanent and loving relationship; nor is male violence convincingly brought under control. Together they find form and expression in the violent punishment inflicted on women who are seen as sexually promiscuous. In short, the failed romance is unable to produce a reading experience in which emotional fulfilment is satisfied through the vicarious sharing of the heroine's journey from a crisis of identity to an identity restored in the arms of a nurturing male. Whether a romance is good or bad is ultimately determined by the kind of relationship the reader can establish with the heroine.

> If the events of the heroine's story provoke too intense feelings such as anger at men, fear of rape and violence, worry about female sexuality, or worry about the need to live with an unexciting man, that romance will be discarded as a failure or judged to be very poor. If, on the other hand, those events call forth feelings of excitement, satisfaction, contentment, self-confidence, pride, and power, it matters less what events are used or how they are marshalled. In the end, what counts most is the reader's sense that for a short time she has become other and been elsewhere. She must close that book reassured that men and marriage really do mean good things for women. She must also turn back to her daily round of duties, emotionally reconstituted and replenished, feeling confident of her worth and convinced of her ability and power to deal with the problem she knows she must confront. (184)

Radway claims that by engaging in this process of discrimination, the Smithton women are taking emotional benefits for themselves where other critics see only financial benefits for the publishing industry. The Smithton women 'partially reclaim the patriarchal form of the romance for their own use' (184). The principal 'psychological benefits' derive from 'the ritualistic repetition of a single, immutable cultural myth' (199, 198). The fact that 60 per cent of the Smithton readers find it occasionally necessary to read the ending first to ensure that the experience of the novel won't counteract the satisfactions of the underlying myth suggests quite strongly that it is the underlying myth of the nurturing male that is ultimately of most importance in the Smithton women's experience of romance reading.

Following a series of comments from the Smithton women, Radway was forced to the conclusion that if she really wished to understand their view of romance reading, she had to relinquish her preoccupation with the text and consider also the very *act of romance reading* itself. In conversations, it became clear that when the women used the term 'escape' to describe the pleasure of romance reading, the term was operating in a double but related sense. As we have seen, it can be used to describe the process of identification between the reader and the heroine–hero relationship. But it became clear that the term was also used 'literally to describe the act of denying the present, which they believe they accomplish each time they begin to read a book and are drawn into its story' (90). Many of the Smithton women describe romance reading as 'a special gift' that they give themselves. It is seen as time reclaimed from the demands of family and domestic duties that they otherwise perform willingly. For this reason, some Smithton men find the very act of women reading a threat to their patriarchal authority. Romance reading is for the Smithton women 'a temporary but literal denial of the demands women recognize as an integral part of their roles as nurturing wives and mothers' (97). And, as Radway suggests, '[a]lthough this experience *is* vicarious, the pleasure it induces is nonetheless real' (100).

> I think it is logical to conclude that romance reading is valued by the Smithton women because the experience itself is *different* from ordinary existence. Not only is it a relaxing release from the tension produced by daily problems and responsibilities, but it creates a time or a space within which a woman can be entirely on her own, preoccupied with her personal needs, desires, and pleasure. It is also a means of transportation or escape to the exotic, or, again, to that which is different. (61)

Romance reading pulls in different 'political' directions, depending on whether the focus is the act of reading or the narrative fantasies of the texts themselves. The first suggests that 'romance reading is oppositional because it allowed the women to refuse momentarily their self-abnegating social role' (210). The second suggests 'that the romance's narrative structure embodies a simple recapitulation and recommendation of patriarchy and its constituent social practices and ideologies' (210). It is this difference, 'between the meaning of the act and the meaning of the text as read', that must be brought into tight focus if we are to understand the full meaning of romance reading (210).

On one thing Radway is clear: women do not read romances out of a sense of contentment with patriarchy. Romance reading contains an element of utopian protest, a longing for a better world. But against this, the narrative structure of the romance appears to suggest that male violence and male indifference are really expressions of love waiting to be decoded in the right way by the right woman. This suggests that patriarchy is only a problem until women learn how to read it properly. It is these complexities and contradictions which Radway refuses to ignore or pretend to resolve. Her only certainty is that it is too soon to know if romance reading can be cited simply as an ideological agent of the patriarchal status quo.

> I feel compelled to point out ... that neither this study nor any other to date provides enough evidence to corroborate this argument fully. We simply do not know what practical effects the repetitive reading of romances has on the way women behave after they have closed their books and returned to their normal, ordinary round of daily activities. (217)

Therefore, we must continue to acknowledge the activity of readers – their selections, purchases, interpretations, appropriations, uses, and so on – as an essential part of the cultural processes and complex practices of making meaning. By paying attention in this way, we increase the possibility of 'articulating the differences between the repressive imposition of ideology and oppositional practices that, though limited in their scope and effect, at least dispute or contest the control of ideological forms' (221–2). The ideological power of romances may be great, but where there is power there is always resistance. The resistance may be confined to selective acts of consumption; dissatisfactions momentarily satisfied by the articulation of limited protest and utopian longing. But, as feminists,

> [w]e should seek it out not only to understand its origins and its utopian longing but also to learn how best to encourage it and bring it to fruition. If we do not, we have already conceded the fight and, in the case of the romance at least, admitted the impossibility of creating a world where the vicarious pleasure supplied by its reading would be unnecessary. (222)

In a generally sympathetic review of the British edition of *Reading the Romance,* Ien Ang (2009) makes a number of criticisms of Radway's approach. She is unhappy with the way in which Radway makes a clear distinction between feminism and romance reading: 'Radway, the researcher, is a feminist and *not* a romance fan, the Smithton women, the researched, are romance readers and *not* feminists' (584). Ang sees this as producing a feminist politics of 'them' and 'us' in which non-feminist women play the role of an alien 'them' to be recruited to the cause. In her view, feminists should not set themselves up as guardians of the true path. This is what Radway does in her insistence, as Ang sees it, that ' "real" social change can only be brought about . . . if romance readers would stop reading romances and become feminist activists instead' (ibid.). Ang simply does not believe that one (romance reading) excludes the other (feminism). Radway's 'vanguardist . . . feminist politics' leads only to 'a form of political moralism, propelled by a desire to make "them" more like "us" ' (585). What is missing from Radway's analysis, according to Ang, is a discussion of 'pleasure as pleasure'. Pleasure is discussed, but always in terms of its unreality – its vicariousness, its function as compensation, its falseness. Ang's complaint is that such an approach focuses too much on the effects, rather than the mechanisms of pleasure. Ultimately, for Radway, it always becomes a question of 'the *ideological function* of pleasure' (586). Against this, Ang argues for seeing pleasure as something which can 'empower' women and not as something which always works 'against their own "real" interests' (881). Radway (1994) has reviewed this aspect of her work and concluded:

> Although I tried very hard not to dismiss the activities of the Smithton women and made an effort to understand the act of romance reading as a positive response to the conditions of everyday life, my account unwittingly repeated the sexist assumption that has warranted a large portion of the commentary on romance. It was still motivated, that is, by the assumption that someone ought to worry responsibly about the effect of fantasy on women readers . . . [repeating] the familiar pattern whereby the commentator distances herself

as knowing analyst from those who, engrossed and entranced by fantasy, cannot know . . . Despite the fact that I wanted to claim the romance for feminism, this familiar opposition between blind fantasy and perspicacious knowing continued to operate within my account. Thus I would now link it [*Reading the Romance*] . . . with the first early efforts to understand the changing genre, a stage in the debate that was characterised most fundamentally, I believe, by suspicions about fantasy, daydream, and play. (19)

Radway cites with approval Alison Light's (1984) point that feminist 'cultural politics must not become "a book-burning legislature", nor should feminists fall into the traps of moralism or dictatorship when discussing romances. "It is conceivable . . . that Barbara Cartland could turn you into a feminist. Reading is never simply a linear con job but a . . . process which therefore remains dynamic and open to change" ' (quoted in Radway 1994: 20).

Since publication of *Reading the Romance* (1987) Radway (1988) has also become critical of much cultural studies work on audiences which, like her own work on romance readers, begins with a particular text and then seeks to demonstrate how this text is consumed. Research projects which are formulated along these lines will 'inevitably begin by assuming that individuals in the audience are already stitched into a particular kind of relation with the [text in question]' (361). As she explains:

Audiences . . . are set in relation to a single set of isolated texts which qualify already as categorically distinct objects. No matter how extensive the effort to dissolve the boundaries of the textual object or the audience, most recent studies of reception, including my own, continue to begin with the 'factual' existence of a particular kind of text which is understood to be received by some set of individuals . . . Users are cordoned off for study and therefore defined as particular kinds of subjects by virtue of their use not only of a single medium but of a single genre as well. No matter how intense our interest in the subsequent, more dispersed cultural use to which such forms are put in daily life by historical subjects infinitely more complex than our representations of them, our practical and analytical starting-point is still always within the producer-product-receiver circuit. (363)

Conducting research in this way, the audience, 'rarely if ever presented as active subjects, let alone as producers of culture' (362), are situated as receivers of whatever 'messages' the text, as the privileged object, has to offer. Radway proposes that we should 'rethink the process of cultural circulation from a new point of view . . . [that is,] from the point of view of the active, producing cultural worker who fashions narratives, stories, objects, and practices from myriad bits and pieces of prior cultural production (ibid.). This would produce a mode of research 'which would focus on the complexities of everyday cultural use' (ibid.). Just as texts are marked by multiple discourses, so are individual members of an audience. Subjectivity is not something fixed and unchanging, it is always on the move, constantly being addressed by, and always taking up, a range of different subject positions. This is subjectivity as nomadic and dispersed. Radway, as a consequence of this recognition, advocates a different research strategy for thinking about the relationship between texts and audiences:

> Instead of segmenting a social formation automatically by construing it precisely as a set of audiences for specific media and/or genre, I have been wondering whether it might not be more fruitful to start with the habits and practices of everyday life as they are actively, discontinuously, even contradictorily pieced together by historical subjects themselves as they move nomadically via disparate associations and relations through day-to-day existence. In effect, I have begun to wonder whether our theories do not impress upon us a new object of analysis, one more difficult to analyse because it can't be so easily pinned down – that is, the endlessly shifting, ever-evolving kaleidoscope of daily life and the way in which the media arc integrated and implicated within it. (366)

This would produce a research practice in which rather than start with the text, it would begin with the lived cultures of people's everyday lives. Therefore, instead of the focus being on, say, the consumption of one specific genre, it would pay attention to how this practice operates in relation to other practices which may in turn, for example, reinforce it or undermine it.

Radway's argument leads to a recognition that consumption is a practice of everyday life. Cultural commodities are not appropriated or used in a social vacuum, such usage and appropriation always takes place in the context of other forms of appropriation and use, which are themselves connected to the other routines, which together form the shifting fabric of everyday life. Roger Silverstone makes a similar point, with specific reference to television viewing, but applicable to other forms of cultural consumption, that we must acknowledge

> the complexity of the social and cultural relations in and through which audiences are embedded. In this sense an enquiry into the audience should be an enquiry, not into a set of preconstituted individuals or rigidly defined social groups, but into a set of daily practices and discourses within which the complex act of watching television is placed alongside others, and through which that complex act is itself constituted. (1994: 133)

Moreover, as Ien Ang argues, ethnographic research of the kind advocated by Radway and Silverstone, has the potential to free research of monolithic notions of the 'audience'. It will allow researchers, she maintains, to see audiences not as an unproblematic given, 'but as a discursive construct, a moving resultant of the power-laden ways in which it is known' (1991: x).

NOTES

1. As Gadamer points out, 'Interpretation is not an occasional additional act subsequent to understanding, but rather understanding is always an interpretation' (1979: 274). In this way, as he explains, 'all interpretation presumes a living relationship between the interpreter and the text' (295).
2. Fish is aware that this opens him up to the dreaded accusation of relativism. This is a charge he strongly refutes, arguing that:

76

everyone is situated somewhere, there is no one for whom the absence of a situational norm would be of any practical consequence . . . In other words, while relativism is a position one can entertain, it is not a position one can occupy. No one can *be* a relativist, because no one can achieve the distance from his own beliefs and assumptions which would result in their being no more authoritative *for him* than the beliefs and assumptions held by others, or, for that matter, the beliefs and assumptions he himself used to hold . . . The point is that there is never a moment when one believes nothing, when consciousness is innocent of any and all categories of thought, and whatever categories of thought are operative at a given moment will serve as an undoubted ground. (319–20)

3. Janice Radway argues that readers of romantic fiction also operate in an 'interpretative community'. How the women read this genre of fiction, she argues, is governed by 'reading strategies and interpretative conventions that the reader has learnt to apply as a member of a particular interpretative community' (1987: 11).

4. Bennett and Woollacott give the example of Ian Fleming commenting on Sean Connery as Bond (Fleming's preferred choice was David Niven): 'Not quite the idea I had of Bond, but he would be if I wrote the books again' (57).

5. See Storey (1992 and 2010) for a discussion of reading formation as a means to understand the consumption of nineteenth-century stage melodrama.

4

FILM

Film studies has generated a wide range of theories and methods. Film has been studied in terms of its potential as 'art', its history told as a series of moments in a 'great tradition', the most significant films, stars and directors; it has been analysed in terms of the changing technology of film production; it has been condemned as a culture industry; and it has been discussed as a key site for the production of individual subjectivities and national identities. This is not, however, a chapter on recent developments in film studies, nor is it even an account of the study of popular film. Rather, the aim is more limited: to discuss a series of key moments in the relationship between the study of film and the development of cultural studies.

STRUCTURALISM AND FILM

In the 1970s, there developed a clear divide within cultural studies between the study of 'texts' and the study of 'lived cultures'. If the object of study was texts, the method of analysis was structuralism. As a result, film studies within cultural studies was dominated by structuralism. In 1975, two important contributions to structuralism and film were published: Will Wright's *Sixguns and Society* and Laura Mulvey's 'Visual Pleasure and Narrative Cinema'. The first is anchored in classical structuralism; the second represents the first significant exploration of post-structuralism and cinema.

Structuralism is a theoretical method derived from the work of the Swiss linguist Ferdinand de Saussure (1974). Saussure divides language into two component parts, which together produce a third. When I write the word 'cat', it produces the inscription 'cat', but also the concept or mental image of a cat: a four-legged feline creature. Saussure calls the first the 'signifier', and the second the 'signified'. Together (like two sides of a sheet of paper) they make up the 'sign'. Saussure argues that the relationship between signifier and signified is arbitrary. The word 'cat' has no cat-like qualities; there is no necessary reason why the signifier 'cat' should produce the signified 'cat': four-legged feline creature. The relationship between the two is simply the result of convention – of cultural agreement. The signifier 'cat' could just as easily produce the signified 'dog': four-legged canine creature. Saussure contends that meaning is not the result of an essential correspondence between signifiers and signifieds, it is rather the result of difference and relationship. The signifier 'cat' means the signified 'cat' because the signifier is not 'mat', 'rat' or 'sat', for example. Language is for Saussure a system of contrasts and opposites.

According to Saussure, then, meaning is produced through a process of combination and selection. Rather than reflecting an already existing reality, the function of language is to organise and construct our access to reality. Different languages will organise and construct the world differently. Inuit peoples are said to have over fifty words to describe snow. Therefore, an Inuet and a European standing together surveying the same snowscape would in fact be seeing two quite different conceptual scenes. What this demonstrates to a structuralist is that the way in which we conceptualise the world is ultimately dependent on the language that we speak and, by analogy, the culture that we inhabit. The meanings made possible by language are thus the result of the interplay of a network of relationships between combination and selection, similarity and difference. Meaning cannot be accounted for by reference to an extra-linguistic reality. As Saussure insists, 'in language there are only differences *without positive terms* ... language has neither ideas nor sounds that existed before the linguistic system, but only conceptual and phonic differences that have issued from the system' (1974: 120).

Saussure makes another distinction which has proved essential to the development of structuralism, the division of language into 'langue' and 'parole'. Langue refers to the system of language, the rules and conventions which organise it. This is language as a social institution. Parole refers to the individual utterance, the individual use of language. To clarify this point, Saussure compares language to the game of chess. Here, we can distinguish between the rules of the game and an actual game of chess. Without the body of rules ('langue') there could be no actual game, but it is only in an actual game ('parole') that these rules are made manifest. It is the homogeneity of the structure which makes the heterogeneity of the performance possible.

Structuralism, as a mode of cultural analysis, takes two basic ideas from Saussure's work. First, a concern with the underlying relations of cultural texts and practices – the 'grammar' which makes meaning possible. Second, the view that meaning is always the result of the interplay of relationships of selection and combination made possible by the underlying structure. In other words, cultural texts and practices are studied as analogous to language. It is the underlying rules of cultural texts and practices which interest structuralists. The task of structuralism, therefore, is to make explicit the rules and conventions ('langue') which govern the production of meaning(s) ('parole').

In his analysis of 'primitive' myth, the French anthropologist Claude Levi-Strauss (1968) claims that beneath the vast heterogeneity of myths there can be discovered a homogeneous structure. In other words, myths work like language. Seen in this way, the anthropologist's task is to discover the underlying 'grammar' – the rules and regulations which make it possible for myths to be meaningful. He argues that myths are structured in terms of 'binary oppositions'. Meaning is produced by dividing the world into mutually exclusive categories: raw/cooked, culture/nature, man/woman, black/white, good/bad, us/them, and so on.

According to Levi-Strauss, all myths have a similar socio-cultural function within society: to resolve magically a society's problems and contradictions. As he contends, 'mythical thought always progresses from the awareness of oppositions toward their resolution . . . the purpose of myth is to provide a logical model capable of overcoming a contradiction' (1968: 224, 228). From this perspective, myths are stories we tell ourselves as a culture in order to banish contradictions and make the world explicable and therefore habitable.

In *Sixguns and Society*, Will Wright (1975) uses the methodology of structuralism (drawing on both Saussure and Levi-Strauss) to analyse the Hollywood Western as myth. His general aim is 'to show how the myths of a society, through their structure, communicate a conceptual order to the members of that society' (17). In particular, he seeks to demonstrate how the Western 'presents a symbolically simple but remarkably deep conceptualization of American social beliefs' (23).

According to Wright, the Western has evolved through three stages: 'classic' (including a variation he calls 'vengeance'), 'transition theme' and 'professional'. Despite the genre's different types, Wright identifies a basic set of structuring oppositions:

inside society	outside society
good	bad
strong	weak
civilization	wilderness (49)

But, as Wright insists (taking him beyond Levi-Strauss), in order to understand fully the social meaning of a myth, it is necessary to analyse not only its binary structure but also its narrative structure – 'the progression of events and the resolution of conflicts' (24). The 'classic' Western is divided into sixteen narrative 'functions':

1. The hero enters a social group.
2. The hero is unknown to the society.
3. The hero is revealed to have an exceptional ability.
4. The society recognises a difference between themselves and the hero; the hero is given a special status.
5. The society does not completely accept the hero.

6. There is a conflict of interests between the villains and the society.
7. The villains are stronger than the society; the society is weak.
8. There is a strong friendship or respect between the hero and a villain.
9. The villains threaten the society.
10. The hero avoids involvement in the conflict.
11. The villains endanger a friend of the hero.
12. The hero fights the villains.
13. The hero defeats the villains.
14. The society is safe.
15. The society accepts the hero.
16. The hero loses or gives up his special status. (48–9)

In the classic Western, the hero and society are (temporarily) aligned in opposition to the villains, who remain outside society. In 'transition theme' Westerns, those that Wright claims provide a bridge between the classic Western, the form which dominated the 1930s, the 1940s and most of the 1950s, and the professional Western, the form which dominated the 1960s and 1970s, the binary oppositions are reversed, and we see the hero outside society struggling against a strong, but corrupt and corrupting, civilisation:

hero	society
outside society	inside society
good	bad
weak	strong
wilderness	civilization (165)

Many of the narrative functions are also inverted. Instead of being outside the society, the hero begins as a valued member of the society. But the society is revealed to be the real 'villain' in opposition to the hero and those outside society and civilisation. In his support for, and eventual alignment with, those outside society and civilisation, he himself crosses from inside to outside and from civilisation to wilderness. But in the end the society is too strong for those outside it, who are ultimately powerless against its force. The best they can do is escape to the wilderness.

In a rather reductive correspondence theory (which undermines much of the strength of Wright's approach), he claims that each type of Western 'corresponds' to a different moment in the recent economic development of the USA: 'the classic Western plot corresponds to the individualistic conception of society underlying a market economy . . . [t]he vengeance plot is a variation that begins to reflect changes in the market economy . . . [t]he professional plot reveals a new conception of society corresponding to the values and attitudes inherent in a planned, corporate economy' (15). Each type in turn articulates its own mythic version of how to achieve the American Dream:

> [t]he classical plot shows that the way to achieve such human rewards as friendship, respect, and dignity is to separate yourself from others and use your strength as an autonomous individual to succor them . . . The vengeance variation . . . . weakens the compatibility of the individual and society by showing that the path to respect and love is to separate yourself from others, struggling individually against your many and strong enemies but striving to remember and return to the softer values of marriage and humility. The transition theme, anticipating new social values, argues that love and companionship are available – at the cost of becoming a social outcast – to the individual who stands firmly and righteously against the intolerance and ignorance of society. Finally, the professional plot . . . argues that companionship and respect are to be achieved only by becoming a skilled technician, who joins an elite group of professionals, accepts any job that is offered, and has loyalty only to the integrity of the team, not to any competing social or community values. (186–7)

VISUAL PLEASURE AND FILM

Laura Mulvey (1975) is concerned with how popular cinema produces and reproduces what she calls the 'male gaze'. The inscription of the image of women in this system is twofold: she is the object of a male desire, and she is the signifier of the threat of castration.

Mulvey's argument is that popular cinema produces two contra-dictory forms of visual pleasure. First, there is scopophilia, the pleasure of looking: 'taking other people as objects, subjecting them to a controlling gaze' (8). Scopophilia also involves sexual objecti-fication: 'using another person as an object of sexual stimulation through sight' (10). In a world structured by 'sexual imbalance', the pleasure of the gaze has been separated into two distinct positions: men look and women exhibit *'to-be-looked-at-ness'* – both playing to and signifying male desire (11). Women are, therefore, crucial to the pleasure of the male gaze. 'Traditionally, the woman displayed has functioned on two levels: as erotic object for the characters within the screen story, and as erotic object for the spectator within the auditorium, with a shifting tension between the looks on either side of the screen' (11–12). She gives the example of the showgirl who can be seen to dance for both looks. When the heroine removes her clothes, it is for the sexual gaze of both the hero in the narrative and the spectator in the auditorium. It is only when they subse-quently make love that a tension arises between the two looks.

The second look is made more complex by the claim that:

> [u]ltimately, the meaning of woman is sexual difference . . . . She connotes something that the look continually circles around but disavows: her lack of a penis, implying a threat of castration and hence unpleasure. . . . Thus the woman as icon, displayed for the gaze and enjoyment of men, the active controllers of the look, always threatens to evoke the anxiety it originally signified. (13)

To salvage pleasure and escape an unpleasurable re-enactment of the original castration complex, the male unconscious can take two routes to safety. The first means of escape is through detailed inves-tigation of the original moment of trauma, usually leading to 'the devaluation, punishment or saving of the guilty object' (13). Mulvey cites the narratives of film noir as typical of this method of anxiety-control. The second means of escape is through 'complete disavowal of castration by the substitution of a fetish object or turning the repre-sented figure itself into a fetish so that it becomes reassuring rather than dangerous' (13–14). Mulvey cites 'the cult of the female star

. . [in which] fetishistic scopophilia builds up the physical beauty of the object, transforming it into something satisfying in itself' (14). This often leads to the erotic look of the spectator no longer being borne by the look of the male protagonist, producing moments of pure erotic spectacle as the camera holds the female body (often fragmented) for the unmediated erotic look of the spectator.

Mulvey concludes her argument by suggesting that the pleasure of popular cinema must be destroyed in order to liberate women from the exploitation and oppression of being the '(passive) raw material for the (active) male gaze' (17). To produce a cinema no longer 'obsessively subordinated to the neurotic needs of the male ego' (18), it is necessary to break with illusionism, making the camera material, and producing in the audience 'dialectics, passionate detachment' (18). Moreover, '[w]omen, whose image has continually been stolen and used for this end [objects of the male gaze], cannot view the decline of the traditional film form with anything much more than sentimental regret' (18).

Mulvey's influence has been enormous. However, some feminists and others working within film and cultural studies have begun to doubt its 'universal validity' (Gamman and Marshment 1988: 5), questioning whether 'the gaze is always male, or whether it is "merely dominant" ' among a range of different ways of seeing, including the female gaze' (5). A particular problem for cultural studies is Mulvey's account of the audience as purely textual – a homogeneous and passive production of the text. There is no room in Mulvey's theory for social, historical subjects who arrive at the cinema with a range of competing and contradictory discourses, which confront and 'negotiate' with the discourses of the film. As Lisa Taylor (1995) notes, 'It is vital to recognise that women are not simply the passive objects of a monolithic "patriarchal ideology", but are actively engaged in resistances and struggles within their everyday lives' (167).

CULTURAL STUDIES AND FILM

Writing in the late 1980s, Christine Gledhill notes 'the recent renewal of feminist interest in mainstream popular culture' (2009:

98). As she also points out, it is a renewal largely happening in opposition to 'the ideological analysis of the late 1970s and early 1980s, influenced by poststructuralism and cine-psychoanalysis, [which] rejected mainstream cinema for its production of patriarchal/bourgeois spectatorship and simultaneous repression of femininity' (98). Rather than the spectator produced by the text, it is interested in 'the conditions of . . . consumption in the lives of sociohistorically constituted audiences' (98). In a Gramscian move, Gledhill advocates an understanding of the relationship between spectators and film text as one of 'negotiation'.

> The value of this notion lies in its avoidance of an overly deterministic view of cultural production, whether economistic (the media product reflects dominant economic interests outside the text), or cine-psychoanalytic (the text constructs spectators through the psycholinguistic mechanisms of the patriarchal unconscious). For the term 'negotiation' implies the holding together of opposite sides in an ongoing process of give-and-take. As a model of meaning production, negotiation conceives cultural exchange as the intersection of processes of production and reception, in which overlapping but non-matching determinations operate. Meaning is neither imposed, nor passively imbibed, but arises out of a struggle or negotiation between competing frames of reference, motivation and experience. (101)

Gledhill suggests that negotiation can be analysed at three different levels: audiences, texts, institutions. Reception 'is potentially the most radical moment of negotiation, because the most variable and unpredictable' (103). As she points out, 'The viewing or reading situation affects the meanings and pleasures of a work by introducing into the cultural exchange a range of determinations, potentially resistant or contradictory, arising from the differential social and cultural constitution of readers or viewers – by class, gender, race, age, personal history, and so on' (103).

Based on research carried out at the end of the 1980s, Jackie Stacey (1994) develops and elaborates this approach. Like Gledhill, Stacey seeks to go beyond the textual determinism

which places women spectators as the passive consumers of the
male gaze. She rejects 'the universalism of much psychoanalytic
work on female spectatorship' (14). Rather than drawing her
conclusions from an analysis solely of the film text itself, she
explores instead the processes and practices of actual women
consuming film. The question which she poses is how women
make sense of what they see and do at the cinema. The specific
focus of her study is the relationship in the 1940s and 1950s
between Hollywood female film stars and British female spectators. She is determined to take 'the audience seriously in an
attempt to counter both the popular and, indeed, the critical
assumption that audiences (especially female ones!) are "passive
dupes" who are easily manipulated by the media' (12).

In particular, she challenges psychoanalytic criticism's account of
female spectatorship as little more than an effect of filmic discourse,
a position and a site produced and addressed by the discourse of
film (see the discussion of Laura Mulvey above). Her study seeks
to go beyond the 'textual spectator' to analyse the responses of
actual women in the audience. To do this, she finds it necessary
to step outside the paradigm of film studies and embrace instead
the concerns of cultural studies. Here is her useful diagram of the
contrasting paradigms of film studies and cultural studies.

Film studies	Cultural studies
Spectatorship positioning	Audience readings
Textual analysis	Ethnographic methods
Meaning as production-led	Meaning as consumption-led
Passive viewer	Active viewer
Unconscious	Conscious
Pessimistic	Optimistic (24)

Stacey's findings are based on research which she carried out on
a group of British white women, mostly aged over 60, and mostly
working-class, who responded to an advertisement which she placed
in two women's magazines, *Woman's Realm* and *Woman's Weekly*,
asking for women to reply if they were keen cinema-goers in the
1940s and 1950s. Those who replied (350) were asked to complete
a questionnaire (238 complied). She organised her analysis of their

letters and completed questionnaires in terms of three discourses generated by the responses themselves: 'escapism', 'identification' and 'consumerism'.

The term 'escapism' is most often used pejoratively, applied to popular culture in order to condemn it as trivial and unworthy of critical or academic engagement. 'Indeed', as she points out, 'this has been particularly true of forms of popular culture enjoyed by women' (90). However, her findings tend to problematise this easy dismissal – suggesting the multidimensional nature of the 'escapism' of cinema-going in the 1940s and 1950s. 'Escapism' is one of the most frequently-cited reasons given by her respondents for going to the cinema. Using Richard Dyer's (1981) argument for the utopian sensibility of popular entertainment, Stacey constructs an account of the utopian possibilities of Hollywood cinema for her female respondents. Dyer argues that entertainment's utopian sensibility is best understood in terms of a series of binary oppositions between problems experienced by the would-be audience and solutions to these problems played out in the texts and practices of entertainment.

Social problems	Textual solutions
Scarcity	Abundance
Exhaustion	Energy
Dreariness	Intensity
Manipulation	Transparency
Fragmentation	Community (177)

However, whereas for Dyer entertainment's utopian sensibility is a property played out in the text or practice, Stacey extends his argument to take into account the total experience of going to the cinema. An analysis of her respondents' letters and answers to her questionnaire make it clear that the pleasures of the cinema were always more than the visual pleasures of the cinema text. She found that besides the obvious appeal of the glamour of the Hollywood stars, other less obvious pleasures included the ritual of attending a screening, the shared experience and community of the audience, the comfort and comparative luxury of the cinema itself. Moreover, each pleasure sustained and secured the others.

Associated as it was with luxury and glamour, in contrast to British drabness at this time, Hollywood was remembered as offering an escape to a materially better world. Thus the specific association of the luxury of Hollywood with the luxury of the cinema interiors at this time clearly contributed to the multi-layered meanings of escapism for female spectators. (97)

In addition, as she points out:

The physical space of the cinema provided a transitional space between everyday life outside the cinema and the fantasy world of the Hollywood film about to be shown. Its design and decor facilitated the processes of escapism enjoyed by these female spectators. As such, cinemas were dream palaces not only in so far as they housed the screening of Hollywood fantasies, but also because of their design and decor which provided a feminised and glamourised space suitable for the cultural consumption of Hollywood films. (99)

She quite rightly insists on the historical specificity of her respondents' escapism. They are not only escaping *into* the luxury of the cinema and the glamour of Hollywood film, they are also escaping *from* the hardships, dangers and restrictions of wartime Britain.

Stacey's second focus is 'identification', 'the relationship between stars and spectators and the processes of the formation of feminine identities through cinematic modes of address' (126). The spectator knows she is not the star, yet for the duration of the film there is a 'temporary fluidity' (126) between her identity and the identity of the Hollywood star. The temporary fluidity is often triggered by a sense of similarity (something shared – hair-colouring, for example). As Stacey explains, 'on the one hand, they value difference for taking them into a world in which their desires could potentially be fulfilled; on the other, they value similarity for enabling them to recognise qualities they already have' (128). Often, identification would extend beyond the cinema to produce what Stacey calls 'identifactory practices' (as distinguished from 'identifactory fantasies'), imitating behaviour and copying appearances.

Stacey is aware that identification is often the key term in claims about female spectatorship made in terms of collusion and complicity. In such analysis, identification is theorised as the successful positioning of the female spectator (as either passive or masochistic) in the interests of patriarchy. However, shifting the focus from the film text to actual spectators in the audience, she finds that the concept of identification undergoes something of a sea change. Although stars may have an ideological function, in that they act as role models in the circulation of normative models of feminine beauty and sexual attractiveness, this is by no means the whole story. Stacey's respondents continually draw attention to the way in which stars can generate fantasies of power, control and self-confidence. 'Hollywood stars can thus be seen as offering more than simple role models of sexual attractiveness (though clearly they offer this too!). However, they were also remembered as offering female spectators a source of fantasy of a more powerful and confident self' (158).

Stacey's final move is to analyse the ways in which her respondents related to Hollywood stars in terms of 'consumption'. Again, she rejects the monolithic assumptions of previous approaches which assume that, in the final analysis, consumption is always successfully located in a relationship of domination, control and exploitation. Without discounting the commodity tie-ins (especially fashion and cosmetics) which formed part of the cinema-going experience (even) in the 1940s and 1950s, and how these might give rise to an analysis which theorised consumption as pandering to the male gaze and facilitating the reproduction of consumer capitalism, Stacey argues for an account which takes seriously 'women's agency as consumers and highlights the contradictions of consumption for women' (185). She insists that 'consumption is a site of negotiated meanings, of resistance and of appropriation as well as of subjection and exploitation' (187).

According to Stacey, 'Film studies work on consumption has tended to perpetuate a very production-led approach to the subject, [taking] as its object of study the ways in which the film industry produces cinema spectators as consumers of both the film and the products of other industries' (188). Focusing too exclusively on production, analysis is never able to pose theoretically (let alone discuss in concrete detail) how audiences use and make meanings from the commodities which they consume. She argues that her respondents' accounts of consumption in the 1940s and 1950s 'highlight a more contradictory relationship between spectatorship and consumption than that presented by the production studies' (190). For example, she notes the ways in which 'American feminine ideals are clearly remembered as transgressing restrictive British femininity and thus employed as strategies of resistance' (198). 'Hollywood stars represented fashions on the screen which were identified by spectators as transgressing restrictive codes of British feminine appearance' (204). Thus the consumption of Hollywood stars and the commodities associated with them was a means to negotiate with and extend notions of British femininity. Many of the letters and completed questionnaires point to the way in which the Hollywood stars represented an alternative femininity, exciting and transgressive. As she explains:

> As well as being vehicles to encourage female spectators to become consumers, and to improve their appearances . . . Hollywood stars were also contested terrains of competing cultural discourses of femininity . . . [T]hey were central to challenges to what was perceived as restrictive British femininity. (205)

Stacey does not argue that these women were free to determine their feminine identities through acts of consumption. But she does insist on 'the importance of maintaining a theoretical understanding of the space between dominant discourses of consumption and female spectators' consumer practices in different locations' (218). Nor does she deny that such forms of consumption may pander to the patriarchal gaze. But as she observes, 'the consumption of Hollywood stars and other commodities for the transformation of self-image produces something in excess of the needs of dominant culture' (223). She contends:

> Paradoxically, whilst commodity consumption for female spectators in mid to late 1950s Britain concerns producing

oneself as a desirable object, it also offers an escape from what is perceived as the drudgery of domesticity and motherhood which increasingly comes to define femininity at this time. Thus, consumption may signify an assertion of self in opposition to the self-sacrifice associated with marriage and motherhood in 1950s Britain. (238)

She concludes that her respondents' accounts of Hollywood stars point to the possibility of 'the use of *American* femininity to rebel against what they perceived as restrictive *British* norms (238). Moreover, she argues, 'The production of a feminine self in relation to Americanness signified "autonomy", "individuality" and "independence" to many female spectators in Britain at this time' (238).

Stacey's approach represents an excellent counter to the universalistic claims of much cine-psychoanalysis. Moving analysis, as she does, from the film text to the female audience, Hollywood's patriarchal power begins to look less monolithic, less seamless. By studying the female audience, 'female spectatorship might be seen as a process of negotiating the dominant meanings of Hollywood cinema, rather than one of being passively positioned by it' (12).

5

NEWSPAPERS AND MAGAZINES

THE POPULAR PRESS

To understand the popular press as popular culture, I think we must learn, from the Norwegian critic Jostein Gripsrud (1992), 'to transcend the futile moralism frequently present in critiques of it'. This does not mean that we must ' "defend" the popular press in any simplistic populist or "anti-elitist" manner, but suggests an understanding of it which differs from the usual lamentations about "commercialism", "vulgarity", etc.' (84).

What are the connections to be made between tabloid journalism and popular culture? Peter Dahlgren (1992) suggests that one 'key link' is storytelling. He sees storytelling as one of the two basic modes of knowing and making sense of the world, the other being the analytic mode. The analytic mode is marked by 'referential information and logic'; the storytelling mode by 'the narratological configurations which provide coherence via enplotment' (14). The official aim of journalism is to present information about the world and is thus a commitment to the analytic mode. However, in practice, it is the storytelling mode which is most often brought into play. Moreover, Dahlgren insists that this is not another way of distinguishing 'between serious and tabloid news, between fact and fiction'; there is between both a 'storytelling continuum' (15).

For Colin Sparks (1992), the key difference between the popular press and the so-called 'quality' press is the mobilisation (by the popular press) of the 'personal' as an explanatory framework. In an analysis of news values, he found that even when the stories in the popular press and the 'quality' press are the same, they are always treated differently.

> [Whereas the] 'quality' press presents a fragmented picture of the world in which the construction of coherence and totality is the work of the reader, the popular press embeds a form of immediacy and totality in its handling of public issues. In particular, this immediacy of explanation is achieved by means of a direct appeal to personal experience. The popular conception of the personal becomes the explanatory framework within which the social order is presented as transparent. (39)

Sparks illustrates his point in a comparison of the respective coverage by *The Sun* and *The Times* of the prison riot in Strangeways jail in April 1990. Although the personal is present in *The Times*'s coverage of the riot, it is not used as the explanatory framework. Instead, the paper attempts to locate the riot 'within a framework which contained different kinds of information and knowledge' (40). The reader is invited, more or less, to make sense of an ongoing series of events. *The Sun*, on the other hand, explained events in 'an immediate explanatory framework in terms of individual and personal causes and responses' (40). Whereas *The Times* presented a range of resources from which to make sense of an event with a past, present and future, *The Sun* reduced the timescale to an unchanging Now, in which certain prisoners did this because other prisoners did that. Although Sparks acknowledges the possibility of 'popular productivity' reworking the meanings presented by *The Sun*, he concludes that 'it seems to me that this is so massively determined a discourse of the "reactionary popular" that it is impossible to rescue it for any conception of progress' (41). The best that can be claimed for the politics of the popular press is that it can 'mobilize a certain ill-defined discontent'. Although it may 'speak in an idiom recognizable by the masses as more or less related to their own [it can] only speak of their concerns, joys and discontents within 'the limits set for it by the existing structures of society' (28).

John Fiske's approach to the popular press is located in the general claim that 'popular culture is potentially, and often actually, progressive (though not radical)' (1989a: 21). He explains the distinction between progressive and radical as follows: '[p]opular texts may be progressive in that they can encourage the production of meanings that work to change or destabilize the social order, but they can never be radical in the sense that they can never oppose head on or overthrow that order' (133).

Fiske distinguishes the popular press from, on the one hand, the official press and, on the other, the alternative press. The popular press is, as he notes, despised by both. According to Fiske, the popular press operates on the borderline between the public and the private: 'its style is sensational, sometimes sceptical, sometimes moralistically earnest; its tone is populist; its modality fluidly denies any stylistic difference between fiction and documentary, between news and entertainment' (1992a: 48).

Fiske's analysis of the popular press begins from Stuart Hall's (2009: 517) claim that the central political division in late capitalist societies is the opposition: '[t]he people versus the power-bloc'. The 'power-bloc' is a shifting alliance of the forces of domination, expressed in and through institutions such as the media, the culture industries, government, the educational system, and so on. 'The people' are also a shifting alliance, defined always in historically specific opposition to the 'power-bloc'. According to Fiske, the official press articulates the interests of the power-bloc in a top-down flow of information. 'A top-down definition of information is', he contends, 'a disciplinary one, and it hides its disciplinarity under notions of objectivity, responsibility and political education. What the people ought to know for a liberal democracy to function properly is a concept that hides repression under its liberal rhetoric and power under its pluralism' (1992a: 49). In other words, the official press, according to Fiske, provide the information and knowledge necessary to ensure the maintenance of the prevailing structures of power. But more than this, it produces what he calls a 'believing subject' (49). This is for Fiske one of the key differences between the official and the popular press.

> The last thing that tabloid journalism produces is a believing subject. One of its most characteristic tones of voice is that of a sceptical laughter which offers the pleasures of disbelief, the pleasures of not being taken in. This popular pleasure of 'seeing through' them (whoever constitutes the powerful *them* of the moment) is the historical result of centuries of subordination which the people have not allowed to develop into subjection. (49)

Fiske uses as an example a recurrent story in the American popular press, that of aliens from space. What interests Fiske is not the main story but its frequent subtheme, that the evidence for the existence of aliens from space and the evidence of UFO landings is being covered up by both the American and Russian governments. What is important here, according to Fiske, is not whether space aliens have or have not actually landed; 'what is at stake is the opposition between popular knowledge and power-bloc knowledge – and it is the opposition, not the knowledge itself, that matters' (49). Fiske contends that such stories stage a 'utopian' assault on the 'normalization' which is essential for the smooth operation of the disciplinary procedures of the power-bloc. The popular press is full of utopian fantasies of another way of understanding the world which challenges the normalising 'reality' of the power-bloc. The popular press produces the sceptical subject who hovers between belief and disbelief, playing thoughtfully in the unresolved contradictions. As Fiske explains, 'recognizing this requires us to view the people as social agents rather than social subjects. The multiplicity of contradictions and their lack of resolution debars any of the coherence necessary to produce and position unified or even divided subjectivities: instead they require active social agents to negotiate them' (53). In effect, what Fiske does is to reverse the claim made by Sparks about the textual difference between 'quality' and popular press. Moreover, the popular press, unlike its official counterpart, makes no effort to present its information to us as an objective set of facts in an unchanging universe: for it, information is not an essentialist knowledge system but is a process that works only in a political relationship to other knowledges. Its politics lies in its oppositionality to the normal, the official. (54)

A key issue for Fiske is relevance. Relevance is not something that can be dictated from above, it is always a production from below. The official press, according to Fiske, using a term from Michel de Certeau (1984), operates with a:

'scriptural economy' which attempts to discipline its readers into 'deciphering' its texts rather than 'reading' them. Deciphering a text is subjecting oneself to its truth . . . reading, however, involves bringing to the text oral competencies developed in the immediate conditions of the reader's social history. Reading is thus a negotiation (typically for de Certeau an antagonistic one) between a text produced from the top and its reading from below. Unresolved contradictions, unstable, unfinished knowledge, scepticism, parody and excess all invite reading: truth and objectivity invite decipherment. Reading is participatory, it involves the production of relevance; decipherment, the perception and acceptance of distance (social and aesthetic). (59)

For the press, popular or otherwise, to become popular culture it has to be taken up by 'the people'; it must provoke conversation and enter oral circulation and recirculation. As he explains, 'Top-down, or official news [for example], has to be re-informed by popular productivity if it is to be made relevant to everyday life' (57). In the final analysis, it is popular productivity which transforms the popular press into popular culture. Like everything else made available by the media and culture industries, it has to be *made* popular.

Ian Connell (1992) takes up a position similar to the one advocated by Fiske. He argues that the popular press, what he calls its 'fantastical reportage', 'sustain[s] certain justifiable resentments' (64). Fantastical or fabulous reportage (as Connell also calls it) does not produce resistance in the form suggested by Fiske. Rather, general discontent mingles with the particular as fantastical report-age 'fuels their resentment of superordinates and all they possess' (66). Stories of the rich and famous falling from grace are the stock-in-trade of the popular press. Instead of resentment against the power-bloc, Connell maintains that:

> Readers engaged by the stories . . . probably want instead all the rewards that [the power-bloc] have granted the fallen heroes of these stories. The main characters of the stories they read have gained, by means made to seem questionable, all the trappings of a good life to which at best they have limited access. I suspect readers recognize the life depicted as good, but desire rather than reject what it can offer. What they are opposed to is their exclusion from it. (66)

Connell argues that media and cultural studies has failed to understand or explain this kind of oppositional resentment.

> Above all what these stories do is mount a populist challenge on privilege . . . While the stories articulate neither a coherent political philosophy nor strategy, their splenetic outbursts do have, however, important political impact. What these stories do is bash the 'power-bloc' – or those representatives of it whose attributes and actions can be most meaningfully represented for their readers. (74)

The 'personalities' of these stories are presented 'as members of a *privileged* caste' (78). Time after time, the details of their wealth and their privileged lifestyles are paraded before the reader. Always mingled in the general narrative of misdeeds is the suggestion that they do not deserve their wealth and privilege. Connell's argument is that the popular press and its readers share a moral economy, a particular set of assumptions about fame: 'It is a status which grants rewards, but it also grants certain responsibilities' (81). This is a morality concerned with the uses and abuses of power and privilege. But, as Connell insists, moral disapprobation is not the main function of these stories. These are above all else political stories in that they articulate relations of antagonism between:

1. powerful elites (from which are drawn the tragic heroes and heroines of the tales);
2. narrators who are by a variety of means in touch with the goings-on of the elites, but who are not at one with them;
3. the rest of us, the powerless ordinary people on whose behalf the stories are told. (81)

The stories articulate a moral economy in which the world is divided between those with power and privilege and those without power and privilege (the 'haves' and the 'have-nots'). At times, there is even the suggestion that those with privilege and power have it at the expense of those without privilege and power. But this is not a radical outrage. Although it offers the pleasure(s) of being a part of an attack on power and privilege, ultimately its resentments are conservative.

> They are not against privileges being granted, merely angry that they have been granted to the wrong people – to 'them' and not 'us', not to 'me'. Their mission is not so much to put a stop to gross inequalities as to redistribute them. Worse still perhaps is the possibility that the populism is a sham. The most vitriolic of the attacks seem to be reserved for those who by good fortune have found themselves one of the stars. They have not been born to stardom. It is, therefore, as if the tabloids are waiting for the inevitable, the moment when these parvenu personalities give themselves away and reveal the ordinariness of their origins. (82)

While Connell insists that this is the case, he also concedes that the stories 'can and do undermine the authority of those who would place themselves apart. They encourage and nourish scepticism about the legitimacy of the class of personalities to act as they do' (82).[1]

MAGAZINES FOR WOMEN AND GIRLS

Angela McRobbie (1991), in an influential essay first published in 1978, argues that *Jackie*, the best-selling teenage girls' magazine in the 1970s, can be analysed 'as a system of messages, a signifying system and a bearer of a certain ideology, an ideology which deals with the construction of teenage femininity' (81–2). *Jackie*, together with other magazines for teenage girls, operates 'to win and shape the consent of the readers to a particular set of values' (82). Like other magazines for both girls and women, *Jackie* promotes 'a feminine culture' (83). Every stage from childhood to womanhood to old age is mapped out in terms of what is expected for the successful fulfilment of femininity. When reading *Jackie*, for example, 'teenage girls are subjected to an explicit attempt to win consent to the dominant order – in terms of femininity, leisure and consumption' (87).

McRobbie identifies four strategies ('subcodes') through which *Jackie* makes its appeal. These are:

1. the code of romance;
2. the code of personal/domestic life;
3. the code of fashion and beauty;
4. the code of pop music. (93)

The code of romance pervades almost every aspect of the magazine. Romance is defined as both serious and fun. 'At the "heart" of this world is the individual girl looking for romance' (98). She is alone and in competition with other girls also alone. Friends are always potential rivals. Happiness is the heterosexual couple. A happy end is a boy and girl together. A girl alone signifies failure. As McRobbie contends, *Jackie*'s code of romance is narrow and explicit:

1. the girl has to fight to *get* and *keep* her man;
2. she can *never* trust another woman unless she is old and 'hideous' in which case she does not appear in these stories anyway;
3. despite this, romance, and being a girl, are fun. (101)

This is a world in which girls must define themselves in terms of their relations with boys. Relationships, other than romantic heterosexual relationships, are not possible. Moreover, the code of romance dictates female passivity. Girls can of course follow the advice of magazines about make-up, dress, and how to act with boys. But true romance only comes to those who wait. Actively to pursue romance (be a 'flirt') is to court inevitable failure.

The code of personal life introduces the darker realm of actuality in contrast to the colourful world of romance. Its principal home is the problem page. Here, as in the world of romance, girls are isolated. The problem page both responds to this isolation and supports and succours it. It is here that we encounter the ideology of the magazine at its most explicit. As McRobbie contends, 'It hammers home, on the last but one page, all those ideas and values prevalent in the other sections, but this time in unambiguous black and white' (111)

The fashion and beauty code encourages girls to see the use of dress and cosmetics as an essential part of being feminine – 'a full-time job demanding skill, patience and learning' (122). According to McRobbie, 'The message is clear. Appearance is of paramount importance to the girl, it should be designed to please both boyfriend and boss alike and threaten the authority of neither' (125).

The code of pop music is not about making music or even about developing an informed interest in pop music; 'the readers are presented, yet again, with another opportunity to indulge their emotions, but this time on the pop-star figure rather than the boyfriend' (126). Girls are invited to look and listen.

McRobbie concludes that *Jackie* functions to map and, ultimately, to limit the feminine sphere. Girls are told how to act and what others expect of them. Their happiness is defined in terms of romantic fulfilment with the right boy. Everything else – including the friendship of other girls – is either preparation for this or an obstacle to be overcome.

Writing in the 1990s, McRobbie (1994) welcomes the fading popularity of *Jackie*, and other magazines like it, and the emergence of new magazines for teenage girls (like *Just Seventeen* and *Mizz*), with an emphasis on fashion and pop music, and attitudes influenced by the success and circulation of feminist ideas.

> *Just Seventeen* has replaced *Jackie* as the top-selling magazine among a female readership aged approximately between 12

and 16. If we look closely at the magazine, it is immediately clear how different it is from its predecessor. Most strikingly, the girl is no longer the victim of romance . . . She no longer distrusts all girls including her best friend because they represent a threat and might steal her 'fella' . . . In fact she no longer exists because the narrative mode in which she appeared three or four times every week, i.e. the picture love-story, no longer exists. Romance is an absent category in *Just Seventeen*. There is love and there is sex and there are boys, but the conventionally coded meta-narrative of romance which . . . could only create a neurotically dependent female subject, has gone for good. (1994: 164)

Janice Winship (1987) argues that 'to simply dismiss women's magazines [is] to dismiss the lives of millions of women who read and enjoyed them each week' (xiii). She contends that a feminist cultural studies must be able to explore the dialectic of 'attraction and rejection' (xiii). As she explains:

Many of the guises of femininity in women's magazines contribute to the secondary status from which we still desire to free ourselves. At the same time it is the dress of femininity which is both source of the pleasure of being a woman – and not a man – and in part the raw material for a feminist vision of the future . . . Thus for feminists one important issue women's magazines can raise is how *do* we take over their feminine ground to create new untrammelled images of and for ourselves? (xiii–xiv)

Part of Winship's project is 'to explain the appeal of the magazine formula and to critically consider its limitations and potential for change' (8). Since their inception in the late eighteenth century, women's magazines have offered their readers a mixture of advice and entertainment. Regardless of politics, women's magazines continue to operate as survival manuals, providing their readers with practical advice on how to cope in a patriarchal culture. This might take the form of an explicit feminist politics, *Spare Rib*, for example, or stories of women triumphing over adversity, say, for example, in *Woman's Own*. The politics may be different, but the formula is much the same.

Women's magazines appeal to their readers by means of a combination of entertainment and useful advice. This appeal, according to Winship, is organised around a range of 'fictions'. These can be the visual fictions of advertisements, or items on fashion, cookery or family and home. They can also be actual fictions: romantic serials, five-minute stories, and so on. Finally, there are the stories of the famous and reports of events in the lives of 'ordinary' women and men. Each in its different way attempts to draw the reader into the world of the magazine, and ultimately into a world of consumption. But pleasure is not totally dependent on purchase. Winship recalls how, one hot July, she gained enormous visual pleasure, without any intention of buying the product, from a magazine advertisement showing a woman diving into an ocean surreally continuous with the tap-end of a bath. She contends that we can 'recognise and relish the vocabulary of dreams in which ads deal' and we can 'vicariously indulge . . . in the fictions they create', while knowing all the time that their promises are probably false (56). Magazine advertisements, like the magazines themselves, provide material with which to dream.

What is really being sold in the fictions of women's magazines, in editorials or advertisements, fashion and home-furnishing items, cookery and cosmetics, is successful and therefore *pleasurable* femininity. Follow *this* practical advice or buy *this* product and be a better lover, a better mother, a better wife, a better woman. The problem with all this from a feminist perspective is that it is always constructed around a mythical individual woman, existing outside powerful social and cultural structures and constraints.

Women's magazines construct 'fictional collectivities' of women (67). This can be seen in the insistent 'we' of editorials; but it is also there in the reader–editor interactions of the letters page. Here, we often find women making sense of the everyday world through a mixture of optimism and fatalism. Winship identifies this tension as an expression of women being 'ideologically bound to the personal terrain and in a position of relative powerlessness about public events' (70). Like the so-called 'triumph over tragedy' stories, the readers' letters and editorial responses often reveal a profound commitment to the 'individual solution'. Both 'teach' the same parable: individual effort will overcome all odds. The reader is 'interpellated' (Althusser 2009) as admiring subject, her own problems put in context; she is able to carry on. Short stories work in much the same way. What links these different 'fictions' is 'that the human triumphs they detail are emotional and not material ones' (76). In many ways, this is essential for the continued existence of the magazines' imagined communities; for to move from the emotional to the material is to run the risk of encountering the divisive presence of, say, class and ethnicity.

> Thus the 'we women' feeling magazines construct is actually comprised of different cultural groups; the very notion of 'we' and 'our world', however, constantly undercuts those divisions to give the semblance of a unity – inside magazines. Outside, when the reader closes her magazine, she is no longer 'friends' with Esther Rantzen and her ilk; but while it lasted it has been a pleasant and reassuring dream. (77)

This is perhaps even more evident on the problem page. Although the problems are personal, and therefore seek personal solutions, Winship argues that 'unless women have access to knowledge which explains personal lives in social terms . . . the onus on "you" to solve "your" problem is likely to be intimidating or . . . only lead to frustrated "solutions" ' (80). Winship gives the example of a letter about a husband (with a sexual past) who cannot forget or forgive his wife's sexual past. As Winship points out, a personal solution to this problem cannot begin to tackle the social and cultural heritage of the sexual double standard. To pretend otherwise is to mislead.

> Agony aunties (and magazines) act as 'friends' to women – they bring women together in their pages – and yet by not providing the knowledge to allow women to see the history of their common social condition, sadly and ironically, they come between women, expecting, and encouraging, them to do alone what they can only do together. (80)

Joke Hermes begins her study of women reading magazines with an observation about previous feminist work on women's magazines:

> I have always felt strongly that the feminist struggle in general should be aimed at claiming respect. It is probably for that reason that I have never felt comfortable with the majority of (feminist) work that has been done on women's magazines. Almost all of these studies show *concern* rather than *respect* for those who read women's magazines. (1995: 1)

This kind of approach generates a form of media criticism, she argues, in which the feminist scholar is both 'prophet and exorcist'. As she explains:

> Feminists using modernity discourse speak on behalf of others who are, implicitly, thought to be unable to see for themselves how bad such media texts as women's magazines are. They need to be enlightened; they need good feminist texts in order to be saved from their false consciousness and to live a life free of false depictions as mediated by women's magazines, of where a woman might find happiness. (ibid.)

Against this way of thinking and working, Hermes advocates what she calls 'a more postmodern view, in which respect rather than concern – or, for that matter, celebration, a term often seen as the hallmark of a postmodern perspective – would have a central place' (ibid.). She is aware 'that readers of all kinds (including we critics) enjoy texts in some contexts that we are critical of in other contexts' (2). The focus of her study, therefore, is to 'understand how women's magazines are read while accepting the preferences of [the women she interviewed]' (ibid.). Working from the perspective of 'a postmodern feminist position', she advocates an:

> appreciation that readers are producers of meaning rather than the cultural dupes of the media institutions. Appreciation too of the local and specific meanings we give to media texts and the different identities any one person may bring to bear on living our multi-faceted lives in societies saturated with

media images and texts of which women's magazines are a part. (5)

More specifically, she seeks to situate her work in a middle ground between a focus on how meanings are made of specific texts (Ang 1985, Radway 1987, for example), and a focus on the contexts of media consumption. In other words, rather than begin with a cultural text and show how people appropriate it and make it meaningful, or begin with the contexts of cultural consumption and show how these constrain the ways in which appropriation and the making of meaning can take place, she has 'tried to reconstruct the diffuse genre or set of genres that is called women's magazines and [to demonstrate] how they become meaningful exclusively through the perception of their readers' (6). She calls this approach 'the theorisation of meaning production in everyday contexts' (ibid.). In working in this way, she is able to avoid the deployment of textual analysis, with its implied notion of an identifiably correct meaning, or limited set of meanings, which a reader may or may not activate. 'My perspective,' she explains, 'is that texts acquire meaning only in the interaction between readers and texts and that analysis of the text on its own is never enough to reconstruct these meanings' (10). To enable this way of working she introduces the concept of 'repertoires'. She explains the concept as follows, 'Repertoires are the cultural resources that speakers fall back on and refer to. Which repertoires are used depends on the cultural capital of an individual reader' (8). Moreover, 'Texts do not directly have meaning. The various repertoires readers use make texts meaningful' (40).

Hermes conducted eighty interviews with both women and men. She was initially disappointed at the fact that her interviewees seemed reluctant to talk about how they made meanings from the women's magazines they read; and when they did discuss this issue, they often suggested instead, against the 'common sense of much media and cultural theory, that their encounters with these magazines were hardly meaningful at all.' After the initial disappointment, these discussions gradually prompted Hermes to recognise what she calls 'the fallacy of meaningfulness' (16). What this phrase is intended to convey is her rejection of a way of working in media and cultural analysis which is premised on the view that the encounter between reader and text should always be understood *solely* in terms of the production of meaning. This general preoccupation with meaning, she claims, has resulted from an influential body of work which concentrated on fans (and, I would add youth subcultures), rather than on the cultural consumption practices of ordinary people; and, moreover, it resulted from a conspicuous failure to situate cultural consumption in the routines of everyday life. Against the influence of this work, she argues for a critical perspective in which 'the media text has to be displaced in favour of readers' reports of their everyday lives' (148). As she explains, 'To understand and theorize everyday media use a more sophisticated view of meaning production is required than one that does not recognise different levels of psychological investment or emotional commitment and reflection' (16).

By a detailed and critical analysis of recurrent themes and repeated issues which arise in the interview material she collected, Hermes attempts to reconstruct the various repertoires employed by the interviewees in the cultural consumption of women's magazines. She identifies four repertoires: 'easily put down'; 'relaxation'; practical knowledge; and 'emotional learning and connected knowing' (31). The first of these repertoires, perhaps the most straightforward to understand, identifies women's magazines as a genre that makes limited demands on its readers. It is a genre that can be easily picked up and easily put down, and because of this, it can be easily accommodated into the routines of everyday life. The second repertoire, clearly related to the first, and perhaps as expected as the first repertoire, identifies reading women's magazines as a form of relaxation. But, as Hermes points out, 'relaxation' (like 'escapism' discussed in Chapter 4) should not be understood as an innocent or a self-evident term – it is, as she maintains, 'ideologically loaded' (36). On the one hand, the term can be employed simply as a valid description of a particular activity, and, on the other, it can be used as a blocking mechanism in defence against personal intrusion. Given the low cultural status of women's magazines, as Hermes reminds us, using the term 'relaxation' as a means to block further entry into a private

realm is perhaps understandable. The third repertoire, the repertoire of practical knowledge, can range from tips on cooking to film
and book reviews. But its apparently secure anchorage in practical
application is deceptive. The repertoire of practical knowledge may
offer much more than practical hints on how to become adept at
making Indian cuisine or culturally knowing about which films are
worth going to the cinema to see. Readers can use these practical
tips, Hermes claims, to fantasise an 'ideal self . . . [who] is pragmatic
and solution-oriented, and a person who can take decisions and is
an emancipated consumer; but above all she is a person in control'
(39). The final repertoire, the repertoire of emotional learning and
connected knowing, is also about learning, but rather than being
about the collection of practical tips, it is learning through the recognition of oneself, one's lifestyle and one's potential problems, in the
problems of others as represented in the pages of magazine stories
and articles. As one interviewee told Hermes, she likes to read 'short
pieces about people who have had certain problems . . . [and] how
such a problem can be solved' (41). Or as another interviewee told
her, 'I like to read about how people deal with things' (42). With
specific reference to problem pages, another interviewee observed,
'you learn a lot from other people's problems . . . and the advice
they [the magazine] give' (43). As with the repertoire of practical
knowledge, the fourth repertoire, emotional learning and connected
knowing, may also involve the production of an ideal self, a self who
is prepared for all the potential emotional dangers and human crises
that might need to be confronted in the social practices of everyday
life. As Hermes explains:

> Both the repertoire of practical knowledge and the repertoire
> of connected knowing may help readers to gain (an imaginary
> and temporary) sense of identity and confidence, of being in
> control or feeling at peace with life, that lasts while they are
> reading and dissipates quickly [unlike the practical tips] when
> the magazine is put down. (48)

Hermes's originality is to have broken decisively with an approach
to cultural analysis in which the researcher insists on the necessity
to establish first the substantive meaning of a text or texts and then

how an audience may or may not read the text to make this meaning. Against this way of working, as she observes:

> [T]he repertoires that readers use give meaning to women's magazine genres in a way that to a quite remarkable extent is independent of the women's magazine text. Readers construct new texts in the form of fantasies and imagined 'new' selves. This leads to the conclusion that a genre study can be based entirely on how women's magazines are read and that it does not need to address the (narrative) structure or content of the text itself at all. (146)

Against more celebratory accounts of women and cultural consumption, Hermes' investigation of the role of repertoires makes her reluctant to see in the practices of women reading magazines an unproblematical form of empowerment. Instead, she argues, we should think of the cultural consumption of women's magazines as providing only temporary 'moments of empowerment' (51).

READING VISUAL CULTURE

Magazines and newspapers consist of more than printed words. Their popularity is unthinkable without taking into account the photographs, the illustrations and the visual advertisements which appear on almost every page. Undoubtedly the most influential work on popular visual culture within cultural studies is the foundational work of the French cultural theorist Roland Barthes.

Barthes's aim is to make explicit what too often remains implicit in the texts and practices of popular culture. His guiding principle is always interrogate 'the falsely obvious' (1973: 11). As he stated in the Preface to the 1957 edition of *Mythologies* (one of the founding texts of cultural studies), 'I resented seeing Nature and History confused at every turn, and I wanted to track down, in the decorative display of *what-goes-without-saying*, the ideological abuse which, in my view, is hidden there' (11).

Barthes's early work on popular culture is concerned with the process of 'signification', the processes through which meanings are produced. He uses Saussure's linguistic model (see Chapter 4)

109

to analyse the texts and practices of French popular culture. He takes Saussure's schema of signifier + signified = sign and adds to it a second level of signification. As noted in Chapter 4, the signifier 'cat' produces the signified 'cat': a primary signification. The sign 'cat' produced in this formulation can become the signifier 'cat' in a second level of signification. This produces at the secondary level the signified 'cat': 'a woman who gossips maliciously' (*Collins English Dictionary*). As the diagram illustrates (Figure 3), the sign of primary signification becomes the signifier of secondary signification. In *Elements of Semiology* (1967), Barthes substitutes the more familiar terms 'denotation' (primary signification) and 'connotation' (secondary signification).

Primary signification Denotation	1. Signifier	2. Signified	
	3. Sign		
Secondary signification	I. SIGNIFIER		II. SIGNIFIED
Connotation	III. SIGN		

Figure 3

In 'Myth Today', Barthes (2009; first published in 1957) claims that it is at the level of secondary signification or connotation that what he calls 'myth' is produced. By myth, Barthes means ideology understood as a body of ideas and practices which defend and actively promote the values and interests of dominant groups in society. Perhaps Barthes's most famous example of the workings of secondary signification is taken from the cover of *Paris Match* (1955). Here is Barthes's account of his encounter with the cover of the magazine:

> I am at the barber's, and a copy of *Paris Match* is offered to me. On the cover, a young Negro in a French uniform is

saluting, with his eyes uplifted, probably fixed on the fold of the tricolour. All this is the meaning of the picture. But, whether naively or not, I see very well what it signifies to me: that France is a great Empire, that all her sons, without colour discrimination, faithfully serve under her flag, and that there is no better answer to the detractors of an alleged colonialism than the zeal shown by this Negro in serving his so-called oppressors. I am therefore faced with a greater semiological system: there is a signifier, itself already formed with a previous system (*a black soldier is giving the French salute*); there is a signified (it is a purposeful mixture of Frenchness and militariness); finally there is a presence of the signified through the signifier. (265)

At the level of primary signification (denotation), this is an image of a black soldier saluting the French flag, while at the level of secondary signification (connotation) it becomes *Paris Match*'s attempt to produce a positive image of French imperialism.

In 'The Photographic Message' (1977a; first published in 1961), Barthes introduces a number of further considerations. Context of publication is important. If, for example, the photograph of the black soldier saluting the flag had appeared on the cover of a socialist magazine, its connotative meaning(s) would have been very different. Readers would have looked for irony. Rather than being read as a positive image of French imperialism, it would have been seen as a sign of imperial exploitation and manipulation. In addition to this, a socialist, for example, reading Barthes's copy of *Paris Match* would not have seen the image as a positive image of French imperialism, but as a desperate attempt to project such an image given the general historical context of France's defeat in Vietnam (1946–54) and its pending defeat in Algeria (1954–62). Despite all this, Barthes is clear about the intention behind the image:

[M]yth has an imperative, buttonholing character . . . [it arrests] in both the physical and the legal sense of the term: French imperiality condemns the saluting Negro to be nothing more than an instrumental signifier, the Negro suddenly hails me in the name of French imperiality; but at the same moment the Negro's salute thickens, becomes vitrified, freezes into an eternal reference meant to *establish* French imperiality. (2009: 266)

Barthes envisages three possible reading positions from which the image can be read. The first would simply see the black soldier saluting the flag as an 'example' of French imperialism, a 'symbol' for it. This is the position of those who produce such myths. The second would see the image as an 'alibi' of French imperialism. This would be the position of the socialist reader to whom Barthes might pass his copy of *Paris Match*. The final reading position is that of the 'myth-consumer' (268). He or she reads the image not as an 'example' or a 'symbol', nor as an 'alibi'; quite simply, the black soldier saluting the flag 'is the very *presence* of French imperiality' (267). There is of course a fourth reading position, that of Barthes himself, the mythologist. This is a reading position from which he seeks to determine the image's means of ideological production, its transformation of 'history' into 'nature' – the way in which the black soldier saluting the flag is made to appear to conjure up *naturally* the concept of French imperialism, to produce a situation in which there is nothing to discuss, it is so *obvious* that one implies the presence of the other. In this way, the relationship between the black soldier saluting the flag and French imperialism has been 'naturalized'. According to Barthes:

> what allows the reader to consume myth innocently is that he does not see it as a semiological system but as an inductive one. Where there is only equivalence, he sees a kind of causal process: the signifier and the signified have, in his eyes, a natural relationship. This confusion can be expressed otherwise: any semiological system is a system of values; now the myth-consumer takes the signification for a system of facts: myth is read as a factual system, whereas it is but a semiological system. (268)

Again, according to Barthes, '[S]emiology has taught us that myth has the task of giving a historical intention a natural justification, and making contingency appear eternal . . . myth is constituted by the loss of the historical quality of things: in it, things lose the memory that they once were made' (268). What is made to disappear from the image of the black soldier saluting the flag:

> is the contingent, historical, in one word *fabricated* quality of colonialism. Myth does not deny things, on the contrary, its function is to talk about them; simply, it purifies them, it makes them innocent, it gives them a natural and eternal justification, it gives them a clarity which is not that of an explanation but that of a statement of fact. If I *state the fact* of French imperiality without explaining it, I am very near to finding that it is natural and *goes without saying* . . . In passing from history to nature, myth acts economically: it abolishes the complexity of human acts . . . it organizes a world which is without contradictions because it is without depth, a world wide open and wallowing in the evident, it establishes a blissful clarity: things appear to mean something by themselves. (269)

Images rarely appear without the accompaniment of a linguistic text of one kind or another. A newspaper photograph, for example, will be surrounded by a title, a caption, a story and the general layout of the page. It will also, as we have already noted, be situated within the context of a particular newspaper or magazine. The context provided by the *Daily Mail* is very different from that provided by the *Socialist Worker*. Readership and reader expectation form part of this context. Barthes contends that 'the text loads the image, burdening it with culture, a moral, an imagination' (1977a: 26). The image does not illustrate the text; it is the text which amplifies the connotative potential of the image. Barthes refers to this process as 'relay'. The relationship can of course work in other ways. For example, rather than 'amplifying a set of connotations already given in the photograph . . . the text produces (invents) an entirely new signified which is retroactively projected into the image, so much so as to appear denoted there' (27). For example, a publicity photograph of a Hollywood actor, taken in 2009 to promote his latest film in which he plays a man who loses a fortune gambling, could be reused to accompany a newspaper report in

2010 about the death of a close friend. The photograph is retitled: 'Cocaine killed my friend'. The caption would bleed into the image, producing (inventing) connotations of loss, despair, and a certain thoughtfulness about the role of drugs in Hollywood. Barthes refers to this process as 'anchorage'. What the example of the different meanings of the photograph of the film star reveal is the polysemic nature of all signs – that is, their potential for multiple signification. Without the addition of a linguistic text, the meaning of the image is very difficult to pin down. The linguistic message works in two ways. First, it helps the reader to identify the denotative meaning of the image: this is a film star looking reflective. Second, it limits the potential proliferation of the connotations of the image: the film star is reflective because of the drug overdose of one of his closest friends. Therefore, the film star is contemplating the role of drugs in Hollywood. Moreover, it tries to make the reader believe that the connotative meaning is actually present at the level of denotation.

What makes the move from denotation to connotation possible is the store of social knowledge (a cultural repertoire) upon which the reader is able to draw when he or she reads the image. Without access to this shared code (conscious or unconscious), the operations of connotations would not be possible. And of course such knowledge is always both historical and cultural. That is to say, it might differ from one culture to another, and from one period to another. Cultural difference might also be marked by differences of class, ethnicity, sexuality and gender. However, as Barthes points out, '[T]he variation in readings is not, however, anarchic; it depends on the different kinds of knowledge – practical, national, cultural, aesthetic – invested in the image [by the reader]' (46). Here we see once again the analogy with language. The individual image is an example of 'parole', and the code of connotations is an example of 'langue' (see Chapter 4). What makes meaning-production possible are the shared cultural codes upon which both the producers and consumers of an image are able to draw. Connotations are therefore not simply produced by the makers of the image, but are activated from an already existing and shared cultural repertoire. An image both draws from the cultural repertoire and at the same time adds to it. Moreover, the cultural repertoire does not form a

114

homogeneous block. Myth is continually confronted by counter-myth. For example, an image containing references to pop-music culture might be seen by a young audience as an index of freedom and heterogeneity, while to an older audience it might signal manipulation and homogeneity. Which codes are mobilised will largely depend on the triple context of the location of the text, the historical moment and the cultural formation of the reader.

CELEBRITY AND PRINT MEDIA

Since the 1980s print media (and other forms of media) have become increasingly dominated by celebrities and celebrity culture. The amount of print space given over to celebrity culture is enormous. In the UK discussion of celebrities dominates the popular press. Similarly, women's magazines have massively increased their focus on the world of celebrities. But most dramatic of all is the emergence of magazines which deal with little else. *Closer, OK, Heat, Hello, Now, OK, Reveal* and *Star,* are all magazines almost entirely focused on celebrities and celebrity culture. Each of these publications, including women's magazines and the popular press, has a particular relationship with the celebrity industries; this can range from being almost sycophantic (*Hello,* for example, often seems to operate like the promotional arm of the industry, enabling and respectful) to being parasitic on, and commercially disabling to, the celebrities they discuss (the *News of the World* is probably the best example of this type of publication). But what is absolutely the case is that the celebrity industries are big business. The promotion of celebrity culture makes money. A celebrity, therefore, whatever else she or he may be, is a commodity produced by the media industries to increase magazine and newspaper circulation and to make profit.

In discussions of contemporary celebrity it is often suggested that this is nothing new, that we can find examples of celebrities throughout history. And of course to a certain extent this is true. But what makes contemporary celebrity different is its apparent ordinariness. The celebrity is no longer a unique being, he or she is now a fundamental feature of everyday life. If in the past a celebrity was someone who became known because of an achievement that might lead to public celebration, today being a celebrity is to be known for being known: it is fame itself that defines celebrity. Even when celebrities can point to achievements in the world of sport or in the entertainment industries, their public visibility will be organised around their private rather than their professional lives. Professional footballers, for example, exist in the world of celebrity for what they do in nightclubs rather than for what they achieve on the playing field. In other words, the achievements of celebrities (if they exist at all) are simply a means to make their celebrity possible, whereas their actual celebrity is a matter of the details of their private lives.

The great paradox of contemporary celebrity culture, therefore, is that it has made celebrity seem ordinary. But how ordinary is the celebrity promoted by the media? Well, it is not very ordinary at all. Media constructions of ordinariness are still representations of a world that most of us will never experience firsthand. The media world of celebrity is an exclusive, hierarchical realm in which our role is to be consumers, invited to applaud and condemn the individuals the media decide to promote as celebrities in what Graeme Turner (2004) describes as 'the destructive cycle of discovery, exploitation and disposal' (84).

But the world of celebrity is more than a marketplace for the promotion and sale of human commodities, it is also a community. Some critics have suggested that the world of celebrity resembles organised religion.[2] Chris Rojek (2001), for example, claims that 'post-God celebrity is now one of the mainstays of organising recognition and belonging in a secular society' (58).

> To the extent that organised religion has declined in the West, celebrity culture has emerged as one of the replacement strategies that promotes new orders of meaning and solidarity. As such, notwithstanding the role that some celebrities have played in destabilising order, celebrity culture is a significant institution in the normative achievement of social integration. (99)

Whether or not the world of celebrity is best understood as the equivalent to a religious community, it is certainly a community in which we are invited to engage in relationships with people we do not actually know (known only to us in media representations). The trick of course is to encourage us to think that we do know them; know them enough to care about the details of their 'private' lives. As part of this strategy celebrities are usually referred to by their first names, giving the impression that we are in fact on first-name terms with them. For example, in August 2009 Kerry Katona, former member of Atomic Kitten, was photographed allegedly snorting cocaine in her family home. As a result she appeared on the cover of most of the UK's celebrity magazines. On each occasion she was addressed as Kerry – 'Kerry Puts Drugs Before Her Kids' (*Closer*, 29 August 2009), 'Kerry's Life In Tatters' (*Now*, 31 August 2009), '"My Life's Over" – Kerry Speaks Out' (*OK*, 1 September 2009), 'Kerry: the pics that ruined her life' (*Reveal*, 29 August 2009), 'Kerry's Meltdown' (*Star*, 31 August 2009). But regardless of the intimate form of address (the use of the personal pronoun) our relations with Kerry Katona, and other celebrities, are always heavily mediated forms of para-social interactions, occurring at a distance with people we do not actually know. But if we focus only on the celebrities and ignore how people consume celebrity culture, and interact in the community of celebrity, we will miss much of significance. For example, although we do not know the celebrities who dominate the media world of celebrity, they can nevertheless function for us as a currency of exchange in communities we build ourselves in discussions we have with other people about celebrities and celebrity culture.[3]

NOTES

1. There may be a similar moral economy operating at the heart of the appeal of television programmes such as *Celebrities Behaving Badly* (Sky).
2. We will encounter similar claims with reference to shopping in Chapter 7. Whether such claims really explain the nature and popularity of celebrity culture, like organised religion, it is certainly a community in which we encounter the ordinary and the extraordinary in close relationship.
3. See discussion of Dorothy Hobson earlier in this chapter.

117

6

MUSIC

Popular music is everywhere. It has become more and more an unavoidable part of our lives. In my youth I had to seek it out. Now it seems to appear everywhere I go. We encounter it in the shopping mall, the supermarket, on the streets, at work, in parks, in pubs, in clubs, in restaurants and cafes, on the television, at the cinema, on the radio, downloaded from the internet on iPods and MP3 players. In addition, we can locate it in music stores, in our individual music collections, on jukeboxes, at concerts and festivals. Our musical choices contribute to our sense of self. They also contribute to the economic well-being of the music industry. In recent times, popular music's undoubted cultural and economic significance has brought it more centrally into the focus of cultural studies.

THE POLITICAL ECONOMY OF POP MUSIC

According to Simon Frith (1983), the work of Theodor Adorno, a leading member of the Frankfurt School, represents 'the most systematic and the most searing analysis of mass culture and the most challenging for anyone claiming even a scrap of value for the products that come churning out of the music industry' (44). In 1941, Adorno published a very influential essay called 'On Popular Music' (2009). In the essay, he makes three specific claims about popular music. First, he claims that it is 'standardized'. 'Standardization', as Adorno points out, 'extends from the most general features to the most specific ones' (63). Once a musical and/or lyrical pattern has proved successful, it is exploited to commercial exhaustion, culminating in 'the crystallization of standards' (67). Moreover, details from one popular song can be interchanged with details from another. Unlike the organic structure of 'serious music' (Beethoven, for example), where each detail expresses the whole, popular music is mechanical in the sense that a given detail can be shifted from one song to another without any real effect on the structure as a whole. In order to conceal standardisation, the music industry engages in what Adorno calls 'pseudo-individualization': '[s]tandardization of song hits keeps the customers in line by doing their listening for them, as it were. Pseudo-individualization, for its part, keeps them in line by making them forget that what they listen to is already listened to for them, or "pre-digested" ' (67).

Adorno's second claim is that popular music promotes passive listening. Work under capitalism is dull and therefore promotes the search for escape, but, because it is also dulling, it leaves little energy for real escape – the demands of 'authentic' culture; instead, refuge is sought in forms such as popular music. The consumption of popular music is always passive, and endlessly repetitive, confirming the world as it is. 'Serious' music plays to the pleasure of the imagination, offering an engagement with the world as it could be. Popular music is the 'non-productive correlate' to life in the office or on the factory floor. The 'strain and boredom' of work leads men and women to the 'avoidance of effort' in their leisure time. Denied 'novelty' in their work time, and too exhausted for it in their leisure time, 'they crave a stimulant' (71): popular music satisfies the craving.

> Its stimulations are met with the inability to vest effort in the ever-identical. This means boredom again. It is a circle which makes escape impossible. The impossibility of escape causes the widespread attitude of inattention toward popular music. The moment of recognition is that of effortless sensation. The sudden attention attached to this moment burns itself out

instanter and relegates the listener to a realm of inattention and distraction. (71)

Popular music operates in a kind of tired dialectic: to consume it demands inattention and distraction, while its consumption produces in the consumer inattention and distraction.

Adorno's third point is the claim that popular music operates as 'social cement' (71). Its 'socio-psychological function' is to achieve in the consumers of popular music 'psychical adjustment to the mechanisms of present-day life' (72). This 'adjustment' manifests itself in 'two major socio-psychological types of mass behaviour . . . the "rhythmically" obedient type and the "emotional" type' (72). The first dances in distraction to the rhythm of his or her own exploitation and oppression. The second wallows in sentimental misery, oblivious to the real conditions of existence.

The political economy of culture has much in common with Adorno's approach. According to Peter Golding and Graham Murdock (1991), two distinguished exponents of the approach, political economy of culture:

> focus[es] on the interplay between the symbolic and economic dimensions of public communications [including popular music]. It sets out to show how different ways of financing and organizing cultural production have traceable consequences for the range of discourses and representations in the public domain and for audiences' *access* to them. [my italics] (15)

The significant word here is 'access' (privileged over 'use' and 'meaning'). This reveals the limitations of the approach: good on the economic dimensions but weak on the symbolic. Too often, political economy's idea of cultural analysis seems to involve little more than detailing access to, and availability of, cultural texts and practices. Political economy rarely advocates a consideration of what these texts and practices might actually mean (textually) or be made to mean in actual use (consumption). As Golding and Murdock point out:

> [I]n contrast to recent work on audience activity within cultural studies, which concentrates on the negotiation of

textual interpretations and media use in immediate social
settings, critical political economy seeks to relate variations
in people's responses to their overall location in the economic
system. (27)

This seems to suggest that audience negotiations are fictitious,
merely illusory moves in a game of economic power. While it is
clearly important to locate the texts and practices of, say, popular
music within the field of their economic determinations, it is insuf-
ficient to do this and think you have also analysed important questions of audience appropriation and use. Political economy threat-
ens, despite its admirable intentions, to collapse everything back
into the economic.[1]

The political economy of culture approach fixes its gaze almost
exclusively on the power of the music industry. Leon Rosselson's
(1979) argument is typical:

> More than any of the other performing arts, the world of song
> is dominated by the money men. . . . The possibility of alter-
> native voices making themselves heard is always small and at
> times, such as now [1979], non-existent. The illusion is that
> song is a freely available commodity. . . . The reality is that
> song is the private property of business organisations. (40–1)

The assumption being made is that the music industry determines
the use value of the products which it produces. At best, audiences passively consume what is offered by the music industry; at
worse, they are cultural dupes, ideologically manipulated by the
music which they consume. Rosselson, for example, claims that the
music industry gives 'the public what they want it to want' (42).
The claim is that how something is produced determines how it can
be consumed. The music industry is a capitalist industry, therefore
its products are capitalist products and, as such, bearers of capitalist ideology.

Rosselson contends that 'folk music' (both because of its origins
in pre-capitalist societies and its contemporary 'anti-commercial'
practices under capitalism) is an alternative music to the capitalist music of the music industry. Pop music 'is incapable of saying

anything valuable about the world in which most people live, love and work' (47). 'Folk music' is offered as a genuine music of 'the people'. How does he know? He knows because of a competition run by the *Sunday Times*:

> [W]hen the *Sunday Times* ran a competition for the best song written about a sporting hero, not one of the thousand entries received used a rock idiom or even the more middle-of-the-road pop ballad. Three-quarters of them used what could loosely be described as a folk or broadside ballad idiom . . . . Clearly, when people have a need to express themselves on any subject other than teenage love, they find no useful model in the rock or pop idiom. The folk tradition . . . is still found to be serviceable. (50)

One might of course wonder whether the readership of the *Sunday Times* and the audience at folk clubs (no doubt there is considerable overlap between the two) provide a fully adequate definition of 'the people'.

There can be no doubt that the music industry has enormous economic and cultural power. But does it follow from this that consumers are totally powerless? As Simon Frith (1983) points out, 'about 10 per cent of all records released (a little less for singles, a little more for LPs) make money' (147). Rather than dictating to a passive market, the music industry finds it very difficult to control the musical tastes of consumers. This is because there is always a difference between exchange value ('economic' value) and use value ('cultural' value). The music industry can control the first, but it is consumers who *make* the second.

Those on the moral and pessimistic left who attack the capitalist relations of consumption miss the point: it is the capitalist relations of production that justify its overthrow and not the consumer choice enabled by the capitalist market. Moral leftists and left pessimists have allowed themselves to become trapped in an elitist and reactionary argument which claims that more (quantity) always means less (quality). Moreover, as Terry Lovell (2009) indicates, the commodities from which popular culture (including popular music) is made:

have different use-values for the individuals who use and purchase them than they have for the capitalists who produce and sell them, and in turn, for capital*ism* as a whole. We may assume that people do not purchase these cultural artefacts *in order* to expose themselves to bourgeois ideology . . . but to satisfy a variety of different wants which can only be guessed at in the absence of analysis and investigation. There is no guarantee that the use-value of the cultural object for its purchaser will even be compatible with its utility to capitalism as bourgeois ideology. (542)

It is important to distinguish between the power of the culture industries and the power of their influence. Too often the two are conflated, but they are not necessarily the same. The trouble with the political economy of culture approach is that it is usually assumed that they are the same. EMI is undoubtedly a powerful multinational capitalist record company, dealing in capitalist commodities. But once this is established, what next? Does it follow, for example, that EMI's products are the bearers of capitalist ideology? That those who buy EMI's records, or pay to see EMI performers play live, are in effect really buying capitalist ideology; being duped by a capitalist record company; being reproduced as capitalist subjects, ready to spend more and more money and consume more and more ideology? The problem with this approach is that it fails to acknowledge fully that capitalism produces commodities on the basis of their exchange value, whereas people tend to consume the commodities of capitalism on the basis of their use value. Commodities are valued for their symbolic significance. Consumption is an active, creative and productive process, concerned with pleasure, identity and the production of meaning. There are in effect two economies running in parallel courses: the economy of use and the economy of exchange. We do not understand one by only interrogating the other.

The situation is further complicated by tensions between particular capitals and capitalism as a whole. Common class interest – unless specific restraints, censorship and so on are imposed – usually take second place to the interests of particular capitals in search of surplus value.

> If surplus value can be extracted from the production of cultural commodities which challenge, or even subvert, the dominant ideology, then all other things being equal it is in the interests of particular capitals to invest in the production of such commodities. Unless collective class restraints are exercised, the individual capitalists' pursuit of surplus value may lead to forms of cultural production which are against the interests of capitalism as a whole. (Lovell 2009: 542)

To explore this possibility would require specific focus on consumption as opposed to production. This is not to deny the claim made by political economy that a full analysis must take into account technological and economic 'determinations'. But it is to insist that if our focus is consumption, then our focus must be consumption as it is experienced, and not as it should be experienced given a prior analysis of the relations of production.

Far from creating and manipulating a passive audience, the various parts of the music industry live or die by their ability to respond to *active* consumption. As Frith (1983) points out, the music industry 'doesn't sell some single, hegemonic idea, but is, rather, a medium through which hundreds of competing ideas flow' (270). Attempts may be made to give some commercial shape to these ideas; but ultimately, as Frith indicates, 'efficient profit-making involves not the creation of "new needs" and audience "manipulation" but, rather, the response to existing needs and audience "satisfaction" ' (270). The music industry may control and determine the repertoire (what music is produced), but it cannot control and determine how the music is used and, moreover, the meaning(s) which it is given by those who use it.

YOUTH AND POP MUSIC

The cultural studies study of pop-music culture begins proper with the work of Stuart Hall and Paddy Whannel (2009; first published in 1964). As they point out, '[T]he picture of young people as innocents exploited by the pop-music industry is over-simplified' (45). Against this, they argue that there is very often conflict between the use made of a text or practice by an audience, and the use intended by the producers. Significantly, they concede that although '[t]his conflict is particularly marked in the field of teenage entertainment . . . it is to some extent common to the whole area of mass entertainment in a commercial setting' (45). Pop-music culture – songs, magazines, concerts, festivals, comics, interviews with pop stars, films, and so on – helps to establish a sense of identity among youth:

> [t]he culture provided by the commercial entertainment market . . . plays a crucial role. It mirrors attitudes and sentiments which are already there, and at the same time provides an expressive field and a set of symbols through which these attitudes can be projected . . . Teenage culture is a contradictory mixture of the authentic and manufactured: it is an area of self-expression for the young and a lush grazing pasture for the commercial providers. (17)

Moreover, pop songs:

> reflect adolescent difficulties in dealing with a tangle of emotional and sexual problems. They invoke the need to experience life directly and intensely. They express the drive for security in an uncertain and changeable emotional world. The fact that they are produced for a commercial market means that the songs and settings lack a certain authenticity. Yet they dramatize authentic feelings. They express vividly the adolescent emotional dilemma. (48)

Pop music exhibits 'emotional realism' (48); young men and women 'identify with these collective representations and . . . use them as guiding fictions. Such symbolic fictions are the folklore by means of which the teenager, in part, shapes and composes his mental picture of the world' (48).

Hall and Whannel also identify the way in which teenagers use particular ways of talking, particular places to go, particular ways of dancing, and particular ways of dressing, to establish distance from the world of adults: they describe dress style as 'a minor popular art . . . used to express certain contemporary attitudes . . . for example, a strong current of social nonconformity and rebelliousness' (49). This line of investigation would come to full fruition in the work of the Centre for Contemporary Cultural Studies in the 1970s, under the directorship of Hall himself. But here, Hall and Whannel draw back from the full possibilities of their inquiries, anxious that an 'anthropological . . . slack relativism', with its focus on the functionality of pop-music culture, would prevent them from posing questions of value and quality, about likes ('are those likes enough?') and needs ('are the needs healthy ones?') and taste ('perhaps tastes can be extended') (50).

Hall and Whannel compare pop music unfavourably with jazz. They claim that jazz is 'infinitely richer . . . both aesthetically and emotionally' (50). They also claim that the comparison is 'much more rewarding' than the more usual comparison between pop music and classical music, as both jazz and pop are popular musics.

> The point behind such comparisons ought not to be *simply* to wean teenagers away from the juke-box heroes, but to alert them to the severe limitations and ephemeral quality of music which is so formula-dominated and so directly attuned to the standards set by the commercial market. It is a genuine widening of sensibility and emotional range which we should be working for – an extension of tastes which might lead to an extension of pleasure. The worst thing which we would say of pop music is not that it is vulgar, or morally wicked, but, more simply, that much of it is not very good. (51)

In the case of classical against pop, the comparison is always to show the banality of pop and to say something about those who consume it. Is Hall and Whannel's comparison fundamentally any different?

SUBCULTURES, ETHNOGRAPHY AND STRUCTURAL HOMOLOGIES

It is through rituals of consumption that subcultures form meaningful identities (see Chapter 7). The selective appropriation and group use of what the market makes available work together to define, express, reflect and resonate group distinction and difference. The classic statement of this process is made by John Clarke et al. (1976) in the first chapter of *Resistance through Rituals*: 'This involves members of a group in the appropriation of particular objects which are, or can be made, "homologous" with their focal concerns, activities, group structure and collective self-image – objects in which they see their central values held and reflected' (56).

One such object is music. Subcultural use of music is perhaps music consumption at its most active. The consumption of music is one of the means through which a subculture forges its identity and culturally reproduces itself by marking its distinction and difference from other members of society. This is not a refusal to recognise the economic and cultural power of the music industry, but an insistence that pop music (like all commercially-provided popular culture) is a contradictory terrain. As Iain Chambers (1985) contends:

> For after the commercial power of the record companies has been recognised, after the persuasive sirens of the radio acknowledged, after the recommendations of the music press noted, it is finally those who buy the records, dance to the rhythms and live to the beat who demonstrate, despite the determined conditions of its production, the wider potential of pop. (xii)

Subcultural use of music was first observed by the American sociologist David Riesman (1990). Writing in 1950, he noted how the audience for popular music could be divided into two groups, 'a majority one, which accepts the adult picture of youth somewhat uncritically, and a minority one in which certain socially rebellious themes are encapsulated' (8). As he pointed out, the minority group is always small. Its rebellion takes a symbolic form:

> an insistence on rigorous standards of judgement and taste . . . a preference for the uncommercialized, unadvertised small bands rather than name bands; the development of a private language and then a flight from it when the private language (the same is true of other aspects of private style) is taken over by the majority group. (9–10)

Thus, consuming a particular music becomes a *way of being* in the world. Music consumption is used as a sign by which the young judge and are judged by others. To be part of a youth subculture is to display one's musical taste and to claim that its consumption is an act of communal creation. It does not matter, according to Riesman, whether the community is real or imagined. What is important is that the music provides a *sense* of community. It is a community created in the act of consumption: '[W]hen he listens to music, even if no one else is around, he listens in a context of imaginary "others" – his listening is indeed often an effort to establish connection with them' (10).

In *Profane Culture* (1978), Paul Willis argues that the 'best ethnography does something which theory and commentary cannot: it presents human experience without minimizing it, and without making it a passive reflex of social structure and social conditions' (170). Ethnography allows the cultural worker to reproduce what Willis calls 'the profane creativity of living cultures' (170). The central concern of *Profane Culture* is the making of culture by 'oppressed, subordinate or minority groups'. Against the common view that such groups are manipulated by the culture industries, he insists that they 'can have a hand in the construction of their own vibrant cultures and are not merely cultural dupes: the fall guys in a social system stacked overwhelmingly against them and dominated by capitalist media and commercial provision' (1). People make culture (in part) through the transformation (what I described in Chapter 1 as 'production in use') of the texts and practices of the culture industries.

As part of his general investigation, Willis studied the music use of two subcultural groups, motorbike boys and hippies. His concern was to explore the 'homologies' between musical selection and taste and other aspects of group lifestyle. Homological analysis is essentially concerned with uncovering the extent to which particular texts and practices 'in their structure and content . . . parallel and reflect the structure, style, typical concerns, attitudes and feelings of the social group' (191). The purpose of homological analysis is to tease out the relationship between the particular cultural choices of a social group and how these are used to construct the cultural meanings of the social group.

Willis found that pop music was an integral part of the culture of the motorbike boys. The music of choice was the classic rock'n'roll of the late 1950s (perceived by the bike boys as a 'golden age' of pop music). Their musical preference ('deliberate choice', not 'passive reception') had 'the dialectical capacity . . . to reflect, resonate and return something of real value to the motor-bike boys' (62). What the music returned was a sense of 'security, authenticity and masculinity' (63). Willis identifies four homologies between the subculture and its consumption of music. First, the historical unity of the music allowed its consumption to mark difference and distinction from those who consumed contemporary pop music. This provided the group with a sense of authenticity. Second, the music, especially early Elvis Presley and Buddy Holly, was seen to validate aggressive masculinity in its celebration (mostly articulated through vocal delivery and the energy of the music, rather than in its lyrical content) of a tough and physical response to an uncertain and uncaring world. Thus the music was seen to have the capacity to make concrete and to authenticate the group's commitment to displays of aggressive masculinity. Third, classic rock'n'roll was perceived as a music of movement (a music with beat) for a lifestyle of movement. Rock'n'roll seemed to articulate the bike boys' sense of a life of endless physical movement. They valued its 'fastness and clarity of beat' (68). Dancing and fast bike-riding are at the heart of this relationship. The pounding rhythm of the music could both incite and supply an imaginary soundtrack to the fast bike-riding of the motorbike boys. Being fast on the road was both a consequence of the music's meaning and a living out of that meaning. Fourth, the motorbike boys preferred singles to albums. The fact a song was not available as a single amounted to a declaration of its worthlessness. For a culture which valued concrete experience over mental activity, listening to albums implied a level of seriousness and musical indulgence foreign to the motorbike boys. Singles put the listener in control; albums implied a commitment beyond the realm of the concrete now.

Willis's investigations of hippy culture revealed the mediating role which drugs, especially acid (LSD: lysergic acid diethylamide) and cannabis played in the consumption of music. It was a common belief that drug use enhanced the appreciation and understanding of music. This view was compounded by the belief (not unfounded) that the principal musicians of the counterculture had themselves experimented with drugs. Drug use was thus seen as a connection between audience and performers: it was the central articulating principle of the hippy culture. It was a culture expressed through the production and consumption of a particular type of music made and consumed in the context of a particular type of drug use. But the coming together (the dialectical interplay) of experiments with hallucinogenics and experiments with making music led to an esoteric (and often elitist) celebration of the very 'meaninglessness' of the music (a refusal of meaning and meaningfulness). It was this which kept the 'secret' at the heart of the hippy culture. 'Straights' were excluded because they lacked access to the 'secret' code, only available through the experience of the dialectical interplay of drugs and music.

Willis discovered that, like the motorbike boys, the hippies were deliberate in their choice of music. The music of preference was so-called 'progressive' rock. Unlike the bike boys, the hippies did not use music as an imaginary soundtrack to fast riding or as a means to engage the body in dance. For the hippies, music was not a means to something else, it was an 'experience' in its own right. Music was for 'concentrated listening'. The hippies interviewed by Willis preferred the relatively uninterrupted flow of an album to the episodic burst of the three-minute single.

A major difference between the two cultures is that whereas the motorbike boys made their culture from a musical repertoire made available to them by the culture industries and had no influence on and interaction with the repertoire from which they made their culture, hippy culture produced the musicians who in turn produced hippy culture. Many of Willis's interviewees knew famous musicians and expected to come into contact with others. As one of his interviewees told him, 'The bands that are producing music today are coming out of this life-style, they are only projecting what we are thinking. They are coming from this life-style, they are growing from us, and they are communicating what we already know' (165).

Willis sees the achievements of both groups in having demonstrated the 'profane' power of subordinate and marginal groups 'to sometimes take as their own, select and creatively develop particular artefacts to express their own meanings' (166).

When we say popular music, we mostly have in mind songs. And if we ask the question 'What does this song mean?' too often we respond by referring to the content of the lyrics. But the meaning of a song cannot be reduced to the words on the page. As Griel Marcus puts it, '[W]ords are sounds we can feel before they are statements to understand' (quoted in Frith 1983: 14). Lyrics are written to be performed. They only really come to life in the performance of a singer.

> In songs, words are the signs of a voice. A song is always a performance and song words are always spoken out – vehicles for the voice ... structures of sound that are *direct* signs of emotion and marks of character ... Pop songs celebrate not the articulate but the inarticulate, and the evaluation of pop singers depends not on words but on sounds – on the noises around the words. (Frith 1983: 35)

The noises around the words – the inability, for example, to find the right words and therefore to make do with everyday language – is the sign of real emotion and sincerity. 'Inarticulateness, not poetry, is the popular songwriter's conventional sign of sincerity' (35).

The celebration of the inarticulate takes many forms. Frith gives the example of soul music: 'the best of soul conviction is the singer's way with non-words' (36). Think of, for example, Otis Redding's struggle to enunciate the right words to express the pain of possible loss in 'I've Been Loving You Too Long' (1965). An analysis based on the song lyrics alone would not be able to capture the emotional force that Redding's performance brings to the song.

This recalls what Roland Barthes (1977b) calls the 'grain' of the voice, 'the body in the voice as it sings' (188). He writes of the need to escape from the urge to search for meaning. The pleasure of music, he argues, is not the pleasure of the representation of something that has happened elsewhere (a reflection of meaning)

131

but the pleasure of what is being made (the making and materiality of meaning). The pleasure and power of popular music is not in the performance of emotion but in the emotion of performance. Barthes's argument is part of a general argument about the difference between 'plaisir' and 'jouissance'. Plaisir refers to 'a pleasure . . . linked to cultural enjoyment and identity' (1975: 9). It is the pleasure of convention and recognition. Jouissance, on the other hand, refers to orgasmic moments of release, beyond meaning. Richard Middleton (1990) gives the example of the difference(s) between Elvis Presley and his contemporary Pat Boone.

> Presley's singing . . . *disrupts* language through a vivid staging of the vocal body, while Boone, marketed as a 'safe' alternative, offers unequivocal meaning in which words, melody and tone fuse into a predictable structure . . . Notice that this is not the same explanation as the usual one – that Boone 'cleaned up' Presley by exorcizing sex; there seems little doubt that Boone's fans heard him as 'sexy'. The difference lies rather in the *way* 'sex' is channelled. To an unusual degree, Presley offered an individual body, unique, untranslatable, outside the familiar cultural framework, exciting and dangerous; in Boone we hear a generalized image, the energy *bound*, tied into the conventional thoughts and sentiments provoked by the words and the intonational rhetoric – safe because explicit and unambiguous. (263)

What Middleton is arguing (following Barthes) is that Presley's performance, unlike that of Boone, goes beyond a performance of the song's meaning. Or, to put it another way, the meaning of a Presley performance is in the performance itself: 'the body in the voice as it sings' producing significance beyond the 'tyranny of meaning'. Presley's performance is not an invitation to meaning and understanding but an invitation to be lost in music, to be overwhelmed by jouissance.

In many ways, this is a distinction between 'performance' and 'message'. It helps explain how one can enjoy songs with politics which one would reject in another context. For example, Simon Frith and Angela McRobbie (1978) derive pleasure from Tammy

Wynette's 'Stand By Your Man', despite rejecting its apparent articulation of patriarchal ideology (4). On a personal note, Barthes's
notion of the 'grain' of the voice helped me to understand my own
pleasure in Bob Dylan's vocal delivery (especially on the albums
recorded in the mid-1960s). I had always (more or less) thought,
until reading Barthes, that my pleasure derived from the lyrical
eloquence of the songs. Yet I could never understand why so many
covers of his material left me cold. Barthes's notion of the 'grain'
seems to point persuasively to the real source of my pleasure.

But denying the significance of meaning in a rush to celebrate
jouissance has its own problems. There is a danger here of cele-
brating pleasure and ignoring politics (see the next section below).
Moreover, to acknowledge that a song's significance cannot be
reduced to its lyrical content should not lead to a dismissal of the
importance of the words altogether.

> Pop lyricists work on the ordinariness of language. They
> make our most commonplace words and phrases suddenly
> seem full of sly jokes and references. With an array of verbal
> bricks and playful clichés, good lyricists, from Bob Dylan to
> Ira Gershwin, add to our sense of *common* language. Their
> songs are about words: they give us new ways to mouth the
> commonplaces of daily discourse. (Frith 1983: 37)

In other words, pop songs have:

> the power to make ordinary language intense and vital; the
> words then resonate – they bring a touch of fantasy into our
> mundane use of them. Pop songs work precisely insofar as
> they are *not* poems ... The pop song banalities people pick up
> on are, in general, not illuminating but encouraging: they give
> emotional currency to the common phrases that are all most
> people have for expressing their daily cares. The language that
> hems us in suddenly seems open – if we can't speak in poetry,
> we can speak in pop songs. They give us a way to *refuse* the
> mundane. (38)

Criticisms of the supposed banality of the lyrics of pop music,
therefore, miss the point. The words of pop music are not intended

to be poetry (and attempts to claim them as such are misguided). Pop music takes the language of the everyday – the cliché, the trite remark, the commonplace – and stages them in an affective play of voice and performance. Again, to quote Frith (1983), the result is 'to make plain talk dance . . . to make ordinary language intense and vital; the words then resonate – they bring a touch of fantasy into our mundane use of them' (37–8).

POLITICS AND POP MUSIC

Politics enters at different moments in the making of pop music: production, distribution, performance, consumption, and so on.[2] At the level of 'common sense', political pop is simply pop that is *political* – pop music which contains an overtly political commentary on the world. In this section, I will attempt to problematise this contention.

Politics is about power, and pop music can be powerful. Politicians have long realised this. They have often dreamed of turning the taste communities of pop music into the voting constituencies of party politics. The prospect of the votes of the young has tempted many a politician into pop music. In 1965, Harold Wilson's courting of the Beatles resulted in their being awarded MBEs. As Robin Denselow (1989) explains, '[I]n his early campaigns he was only too pleased to be photographed puffing his pipe alongside these charming, cute and utterly safe-seeming mop-tops who were working such wonders for the British balance of payments' (92). Of course, the relationship soured somewhat in 1969, when John Lennon returned his award in protest at Britain's support for America's war in Vietnam. But while it lasted, it was political pop. There are many other illustrations of such relationships. Jimmy Carter tried to use Bob Dylan, both Ronald Reagan and Walter Mondale tried to use Bruce Springsteen, and Neil Kinnock appeared in a Tracy Ullman video. All are examples of political pop.

Politicians involve themselves in pop music in other ways – for example, the demand for censorship. In 1977, the year of the Royal Silver Jubilee, pressure was exerted to ban the Sex Pistols' 'God Save The Queen'. The song was banned and went straight to

134

number one. In other countries, censorship is much more harshly implemented. In pre-democratic South Africa, all lyric sheets had to be submitted for official scrutiny before a song could be recorded. These are both instances of political pop.

Pop can be political if the musicians say it is. Taste communities can become political constituencies. West Coast rock was ideologically premised on opposition to America's war in Vietnam. It addressed its audience as actual or potential members of an 'alternative' society. Part of the sense of belonging involved an attitude to the Vietnam War. The prevalence of this anti-war feeling was such that, in the context of the counterculture, all songs were in a sense against the war. The fact that Country Joe and the Fish sang songs against the war was enough to make all their songs seem implicitly against the war. Opposition to the war was the central articulating principle of the counterculture: music both expressed the values and aspirations of the counterculture, while at the same time it helped consolidate and reproduce the culture. This is another example of political pop.

Sometimes the situation is more complex. For example, on their 1985 American tour, U2 found they had to explain the politics of their song 'Sunday, Bloody Sunday'. In performance after performance, Bono attacked what he regarded as the senseless politics of Irish Americans who constantly referred to 'the war back home' with enthusiasm and excitement. 'Sunday, Bloody Sunday', he explained, is not a song in celebration of the IRA. Yet, despite Bono's protests to the contrary, the audience seemed determined to claim it for the American version of the Irish Revolution – in other words, to claim it as political pop.

The music industry has its own definition of political pop music: political pop as sales category. Certain pop – rap, or the work of Billy Bragg, for example – is marketed as political. Since the mid-1960s, record companies have been comfortably making money out of politics. By 1968, the music of the counterculture had begun to be marketed under slogans such as 'The revolutionaries are on Columbia'; 'Psychedelia – the sound of the NOW generation' (MGM). This is incorporation on a grand scale. When it comes to individual songs, their attitude is often quite different. Selling the music of a subculture, or of a particular genre, or even the work of a particular performer, as political is fine, but selling the individual political song is something quite different. In the unpredictable and ever-changing world of pop-music culture, individual political songs (cut loose from a movement, a genre, a profitable performer) are something that record companies would rather not handle. The big transnational record companies universalise their interests and profits by dealing in universals. The politics of profit which try to dictate the terms of the international market consider the political pop song to be too specific to make money. From the perspective of the music industry, political pop, unless it can be catalogued in a particular way, is financially far too risky. At home, these risks are of offending, of seeming too opinionated, of crossing the line between entertainment and dull social comment. Abroad, the risks are that the audience will not connect with the ideas and experiences dealt with in the song. Political pop (as defined by the industry) is a financial risk.

Another definition of political pop music is pop music *organised* politically. In 1976, Eric Clapton voiced his support for Enoch Powell's racism. Outrage within pop quickly solidified into the anti-racist umbrella organisation, Rock Against Racism (RAR). RAR was a united pop collective which staged concerts and festivals. Together with the Anti-Nazi League, RAR was successful in curbing the growth of organised racism. Political pop in the 1980s (using this definition) began with the release of the 'No Nukes' film and triple album featuring the performances of members of Musicians United For Safe Energy. The Sun City Project, established in 1985, united pop musicians in opposition to apartheid in a declared refusal to play the Sun City entertainment complex in South Africa. The result was a single, a video and an album. Live Aid, perhaps the key political pop event of the 1980s, reached an audience in excess of two billion. It gave famine both money and publicity. The following year, Amnesty International's Conspiracy of Hope tour played for a week across America from San Francisco to New York. As a result, Amnesty International doubled its membership in the USA. Two years later, it organised the Amnesty International World Tour. Using pop music to establish constituencies for specific political campaigns makes pop music political. We can of course be cynical and suggest that some of the performers who have supported political campaigns have done so simply to sell records. Well-founded or not, such cynicism *should* not survive the witnessing of the deeply moving reception accorded to Nelson Mandela at Wembley in April 1990. However the performers were defining their presence that day, the audience clearly wanted to be part of a utopian-political moment when pop music mattered enough for the world's most famous political prisoner (released only two months earlier) to thank a pop-music audience because they 'chose to care'.

To call pop music political is to bring into play a diversity of meanings. Pop music can be political *simultaneously* in lots of different ways. As John Street (1986) puts it, '[T]he politics of music are a mixture of state policies, business practices, artistic choices and audience responses' (23). Each of these elements places restrictions on and offers possibilities for the politics of pop music.

NOTES

1. The political economy of culture approach puts most of its considerable critical energy into the moment of production. The moment of consumption is seen very much as a secondary moment. But as Karl Marx, from whom much of the authority of the approach derives, argues, '[C]onsumption produces production . . . because a product . . . unlike a mere natural object, proves itself to be, becomes a product only through consumption' (1973: 91).
2. This section is based on research carried out by myself and Debbie Johnson. For a full account, see Storey and Johnson (1994).

7

CONSUMPTION IN EVERYDAY LIFE

Cultural studies is concerned with the study of consumption for two reasons. The first is a theoretical reason. To know how 'texts' are *made to mean* requires a consideration of consumption. This will take us beyond an interest in the meaning of a 'text' (that is, meaning as something 'essential', inscribed and guaranteed), to a focus on the range of meanings that a 'text' makes possible (that is, its 'social' meanings, how it is appropriated and used in the consumption practices of everyday life). This point is often missed in critiques of ethnographic work in cultural studies. Cultural studies ethnography is not a means to verify the 'true' meaning or meanings of a 'text'; rather, ethnographic investigation is undertaken as a means to discover the meanings people make; the meanings which circulate and become embedded in the lived cultures of people's everyday lives.

We tend to think of consumption as something of recent origin. But, as historian Ann Bermingham (1995) observes:

> [O]ne of the most extraordinary aspects of mass consumption since the seventeenth century, and perhaps the thing that distinguishes the modern period from any that preceded it,

is the fact that consumption has been the primary means through which individuals have participated in culture and transformed it. (14)

Moreover, as another historian Joyce Appleby (1993) points out, such histories should show to be totally inadequate the claim:

> that ordinary people – the masses – consume because they have been infected with artificial wants dreamed up by the international league of producers, [nor would it be adequate to] treat it [consumption] as a residual category – what people do when they are blocked from nobler activities like philanthropy, meaningful politics and becoming mature. (247)

Against such a position Amanda Vickery argues for a view of consumption 'as a positive contribution to the creation of culture and meaning' (278). In her own research she seeks to 'move beyond the moment of purchase', to the way goods are 'used and the multitude of meanings invested in possessions over time' as they are placed in new contexts and in new relationships with other goods (281, 282). It is important, she maintains, if we are fully to understand consumption, that we try to track items as they enter the personal economy of the consumer, where they may be given new meanings, as they are placed in shifting contexts and changing relationships; and they become part of the processes she calls '*inconspicuous* consumption' (284). As an example of these processes she cites research she carried out on Ellen Weeton Stock, a woman who worked as a governess in early nineteenth-century Lancashire. In a letter to her daughter Mary, written to accompany a number of family heirlooms, Stock wrote:

> The green ribbon is part of a boxfull my mother once had; they were taken in a prize which my father captured during the American war. . . . The piece of patchwork is an old quilt, I made it about 20 years ago; the hexagon in the middle was of our best bed hangings . . . they were chintzs my father brought home with him from one of his voyages. . . . I am thus minded, my Mary, that you might know something of the history of your mother's family. (quoted in Vickery 1993: 293–4)

The second reason cultural studies is concerned with consumption is political. Cultural studies has always rejected the 'pessimistic elitism' which haunts so much work in cultural theory and analysis (I have in mind Leavisism, the Frankfurt School, most versions of structuralism, 'economistic' versions of Marxism, political economy) which always seem to want to suggest that 'agency' is overwhelmed by 'structure'; that consumption is a mere shadow of production; that audience negotiations are fictions, merely illusory moves in a game of economic power (Storey 1999). Moreover, 'pessimistic elitism' is a way of thinking which seeks to present itself as a form of radical cultural politics. But too often this is a politics in which attacks on power are rarely little more than self-serving revelations about how 'other people' are always 'cultural dupes'.

Although cultural studies recognises that the capitalist culture industries are a major site of ideological production, constructing powerful images, descriptions, definitions, frames of reference for understanding the world, cultural studies rejects the view that to consume these productions is to become the hopeless victim of 'false consciousness' (whether capitalist, imperialist, patriarchal, or heteronormative). Although we should never lose sight of the manipulative powers of capital and the authoritarian, and authoring, structures of production, we must insist on the active complexity, and situated agency, of consumption. Culture is not something already made which we consume; culture is what we *make* in the varied practices of everyday life, including consumption. Consumption involves the *making* of culture; this is why it matters (Miller 1987, Storey 1999). Moreover, it is a central argument of cultural studies that making culture is complex and contradictory, and cannot be explained by simple notions of determination and manipulation. This is not to say that consumption is always empowering and resistant. To deny the passivity of consumption is not to deny that sometimes consumption is passive; to deny that the consumers of the commodities produced by the capitalist culture industries are cultural dupes is not to deny that the capitalist culture industries seek to manipulate. But it is to deny that the cultures of everyday life are little more than degraded landscapes of commercial and ideological manipulation, imposed from above in order to make profit and secure social control. Cultural studies insists that to decide on these matters requires vigilance and attention to the details of the active relations between production and consumption. These are not matters that can be decided once and for all (outside the contextual contingencies of history and politics) with an elitist glance and a condescending sneer. Nor can they be read off from the moment of production (locating meaning, pleasure, ideological effect, incorporation, resistance, in, variously, the intention, the means of production or the production itself): these are only the 'pre-texts' for consumption as 'production in use'; and it is, ultimately, in 'production in use' that questions of meaning, pleasure, ideological effect, incorporation or resistance, can be (contextually and contingently) decided.

SUBCULTURAL CONSUMPTION

It is in work on youth subcultures that the cultural studies engagement with consumption begins. More specifically, it begins with Phil Cohen's (1980; first published in 1972) foundational analysis of working-class culture and youth subcultures in the East End of London. Cohen contends that youth subcultures are an attempt to solve problems experienced by the parent culture (the working-class culture of parents, non-subcultural peers, and so on). From the mid-1950s onwards, the working class had been confronted by two contradictory discourses: the new ideology of affluence and 'conspicuous consumption' and the traditional claims of working-class life. Changes in local manufacturing (resulting in 'de-skilling') and changes in the local environment (high-rise flats) had together undermined traditional working-class life without increasing access to the new 'affluent society'.

> It seems to me that the latent function of subculture is this: to express and resolve, albeit 'magically', the contradictions which remain hidden or unresolved in the parent culture. The succession of subcultures which this parent culture generated can thus all be considered so many variations on a central theme – the contradiction, at an ideological level, between

141

traditional working-class puritanism and the new hedonism of consumption; at an economic level, between a future as part of the socially mobile elite or as part of the new lumpen proletariat. Mods, parkas, skinheads, crombies all represent, in their different ways, an attempt to retrieve some of the socially cohesive elements destroyed in their parent culture and to combine these with elements selected from other class fractions, symbolizing one or other of the options confronting it. (82–3)

In other words, in a symbolic response to the break-up of traditional working-class culture, a succession of youth subcultures attempted to hold together traditional notions of working-class community, while at the same time taking part (through acts of selective appropriation and consumption) in the opportunities presented by the 'affluent society'. For example, although mods tended to be employed in low-paid work, with few career opportunities, the style of the mod could be seen to represent 'an attempt to realise, but in an *imaginary relation* the conditions of existence of the socially mobile white collar worker' (82). Similarly, although they shared many of the traditional values of their parent culture ('their argot and ritual forms'), 'their dress and music reflected the hedonistic image of the affluent consumer' (83). Thus subcultures represent 'a compromise solution to two contradictory needs: the need to create and express *autonomy* and *difference* from parents . . . and the need to maintain . . . *parental identifications*' (84). Or, as Dick Hebdige (1979) explains it:

> [M]ods were negotiating changes and contradictions which were simultaneously affecting the parent culture but they were doing so in the terms of their own relatively autonomous problematic – by inventing an 'elsewhere' (the week-end, the West End) which was defined *against* the familiar locales of the home, the pub, the working-man's club, the neighbourhood. (79)

John Clarke et al. (1976) elaborate Cohen's approach by situating youth subcultures in terms of both the parent culture and the dominant culture. Following Cohen's lead, they approach youth subcultures as 'coded' representations of conflicts and contradictions affecting the working class as a whole. Using Gramsci's theory of hegemony, they argue that the struggles of youth subcultures should be located in the wider class struggle. Hebdige (1979) shifts the emphasis from class politics to the politics of style. As he explains, '[T]he challenge to hegemony which subcultures represent is not issued directly by them. Rather it is expressed obliquely, in style' (17). For example, in an earlier discussion of subcultures, Hebdige (1976) claims of mod style:

> The style they created . . . constituted a parody of the consumer society in which they were situated. The mod dealt his blows by inverting and distorting the images (of neatness, of short hair) so cherished by his employers and parents, to create a style, which while being overtly close to the straight world was nonetheless incomprehensible to it. (93)

Youth subcultures communicate through acts of consumption. As Hebdige maintains, youth subcultures are 'concerned first and foremost with consumption' (Hebdige 1979: 94–5).

> They are . . . cultures of conspicuous consumption – even when, as with the skinheads and the punks, certain types of consumption are conspicuously refused – and it is through the distinctive rituals of consumption, through style, that the subculture at once reveals its 'secret' identity and communicates its forbidden meanings. It is basically the way in which commodities are *used* in subculture which mark the subculture off from more orthodox cultural formations. (102–3)

Subcultural consumption is consumption at its most discriminating. Through a process of 'bricolage', subcultures appropriate for their own purposes and meanings the commodities commercially provided. Products are combined or transformed in ways not intended by their producers; commodities are rearticulated to produce oppositional meanings. Examples include teddy boys wearing Savile Row Edwardian jackets, mods wearing Italian suits, punks using bin-liners and safety pins. In this way (and through patterns of behaviour, ways of speaking, taste in music, and so on), youth subcultures engage in symbolic forms of resistance to both dominant and parent cultures. According to this model, youth subcultures always move from originality and opposition to commercial incorporation and ideological defusion as the culture industries eventually succeed in marketing subcultural resistance for general consumption and profit. As Hebdige explains, 'Youth cultural styles may begin by issuing symbolic challenges, but they must end by establishing new sets of conventions; by creating new commodities, new industries or rejuvenating old ones' (96).

The approach to youth subcultures (from Cohen to Hebdige) has been challenged from *within* cultural studies on two counts. First, as Angela McRobbie and Jenny Garber (1976) asked, 'Are girls ... *really* not active or present in youth subcultures? Or has something in the way this research is done rendered them invisible?' (209). The answer to the first question is that girls are active but often in different ways from boys. The answer to the second question was yes.

The introduction of gender has broadened the focus of cultural studies work on youth subcultures. For example, Angela McRobbie has introduced dance into cultural studies. Writing in 1984, she claims that 'when dance has found its way into accounts of working-class culture, it has tended to be either derided as trivial or else taken as a sign of moral degeneration' (1991: 132). She cites Richard Hoggart's *The Uses of Literacy* (first published in 1957), in which dancing is seen as just one part of a culture of femininity which is 'flighty, careless and inane' (Hoggart 1990: 51).

Dance is a form of artistic practice but it is also a social practice, a leisure activity, a ritual form of sexuality, a method of exercise and a means of communication, 'a way of speaking through the body' (McRobbie 1991: 195). According to McRobbie, 'Dance for girls represents a public extension of the private culture of femininity which takes place outside the worried gaze of the moral guardians and indoors in the protected space of the home' (197). Although she is fully aware that dance can be a means of conforming to social expectations of femininity, an appropriate means to instil in girls the 'feminine' attributes of grace and control, she nevertheless insists that:

> dance carries enormously pleasurable qualities for girls and women which frequently seem to suggest a displaced, shared and nebulous eroticism rather than a straightforwardly romantic, heavily heterosexual 'goal-oriented' drive. As a purveyor of fantasy, dance has also addressed areas of absolute privacy and personal intimacy, especially important for women and girls. And there is I think a case which can be made for forms of fantasy, daydreaming, and 'abandon' to be interpreted as part of a strategy of resistance or opposition; that is, as marking out one of those areas which cannot be totally colonised. Dance and music play an important role in these small daily *evasions*, partly because they are so strongly inscribed, in our culture, within the realms of feeling and emotion. They are associated with being temporarily out of control, or out of the reaches of controlling forces. (134)

Moreover, dance offers 'the opportunity for fantasy' (144). Like the spectator in the darkness of the cinema, 'the dancer can retain some degree of anonymity or absorption . . . blotting-out of the self, a suspension of real, daylight consciousness, and an aura of dream-like self-reflection' (144). However, there is an important difference between the fantasy afforded by cinema and that realised through dance. As McRobbie explains:

> [C]inema offers a one-way fantasy which is directed solely through the gaze of the spectator towards the screen, the fantasy of dancing is more social, more reciprocated. This is because it allows simultaneously a dramatic display of the self and the body, with an equally dramatic negation of the self and the body. (144)

A second series of objections concerns the way in which much early subcultural analysis presents those outside a subculture. Subcultural analysis always tends to celebrate the extraordinary as against the ordinary. Subcultures represent youth in resistance, actively refusing to conform to the supposed passive commercial tastes of the majority of youth. Once resistance has given way to incorporation, analysis stops, waiting for the next 'great refusal'. The move from subcultures to the consumption patterns of young people as a whole was developed around the recognition that all young people are active consumers of culture and not the passive cultural dupes of much subcultural theory. As Angela McRobbie (1994) explains:

> While in the early days of subcultural theory from the Centre for Contemporary Cultural Studies (CCCS) it was important to draw a line between youth culture and pop culture, crediting the former with a form of symbolic class authenticity and the latter with all the marks of the consumer culture, in reality the two were always merged, involved in an ongoing relationship. (156)

This recognition was part of a general move away from an 'elitist' view of youth culture organised around a binary opposition between resistant 'style' and conformist 'fashion', but it was also governed by an apparent breakdown of (or at the very least, a blurring of) the distinction between the two. According to McRobbie, the change 'reflected a situation in which youthfulness became virtually synonymous with subculture' (159), as subcultures proliferated and were recycled.

Gary Clarke (1990; first published 1981) also rejects the 'dichotomy between subcultures and ... the rest of society as being straight, incorporated in a consensus, and willing to scream undividedly loud in any moral panic' (84). He also objects to the London-centredness of much subcultural theory and its suggestion that the appearance of a given youth subculture in the provinces is a telling sign of the subculture's incorporation (86). At the centre of Clarke's critique is a suspicion of the presence of an implicit cultural elitism structuring much subcultural theory.

> I would argue generally that the subcultural literature's focus on the stylistic deviance of a few contains (albeit implicitly) a similar treatment of the rest of the working class as unproblematically incorporated. This is evident, for example,

in the distaste felt for youth deemed as outside subcultural activity – even though most 'straight' working-class youths enjoy the same music, styles, and activities as the subcultures – and in the disdain for such cults as glam, disco, and the ted revival, which lack 'authenticity'. Indeed, there seems to be an underlying contempt for 'mass culture' (which stimulates the interest in those who deviate from it) which stems from the work of the Marxism of the Frankfurt School and, within the English tradition, to the fear of mass culture expressed in *The Uses of Literacy*. (90)

If subcultural consumption is to remain an area of concern in cultural studies, Clarke suggests that future analysis 'should take the breakthrough of a style as its starting point' (92). Better still, cultural studies should focus on 'the activities of all youths to locate continuities and discontinuities in culture and social relations and to discover the meaning these activities have for the youths themselves' (95).

FAN CULTURES AND TEXTUAL POACHING

In *The Practice of Everyday Life*, the French cultural theorist Michel de Certeau (1984) is concerned with what he calls the 'ways of operating' of ordinary consumers as they move across the dominated landscape of cultural production. As he explains:

> The purpose of this work is to make explicit the systems of operational combination (les combinatoires d'opérations) which also compose a 'culture', and to bring to light the models of action characteristic of users whose status as the dominated element in society (a status that does not mean that they are either passive or docile) is concealed by the euphemistic term 'consumers'. Everyday life invents itself by *poaching* in countless ways on the property of others. (xi–xii)

He seeks to deconstruct the term 'consumer', to reveal the activity which lies within the act of consumption or what he prefers to call 'secondary production'. Consumption, he argues, 'is devious, it is dispersed, but it insinuates itself everywhere, silently and almost invisibly, because it does not manifest itself through its own products, but rather through its ways of using the products imposed by a dominant economic order' (xii–xiii). De Certeau offers the example of the ways in which indigenous Indians of what is now South America, 'subverted from within' (xiii) the Spanish colonisers' imposed culture:

> Submissive, and even consenting to their subjection, the Indians nevertheless often *made of* the rituals, representations, and laws imposed on them something quite different from what their conquerors had in mind; they subverted them not by rejecting or altering them, but by using them with respect to ends and references foreign to the system they had no choice but to accept. (ibid.)

In this way, 'their use of the dominant social order deflected its power, which they lacked the means to challenge'; and, as de Certeau observes, 'they escaped it without leaving it. The strength of their difference lay in procedures of "consumption" ' (ibid.). Another example of the same process of subversion from within can be seen in the experience of the Africans who were enslaved and transported to the USA to work on the cotton plantations. As part of the process of instilling submission, the slaves were taught Christianity. As in de Certeau's example of Indians resisting Spanish culture, the slaves consumed and *used* the new religion as a means to think of the possibilities of their own freedom. In other words, a religion which should have reconciled them to their position as slaves was used in such a way as to enable them not only to think outside the brutal confines of slavery, but was also used to think through the challenges and confrontations of the Civil Rights movement and beyond.

For de Certeau, the terrain of culture is a site of continual conflict (silent and almost invisible) between the 'strategies' of cultural imposition (the power of production) and the 'tactics' of cultural use (consumption or 'secondary production'). The difference between the two is that 'strategies are able to produce . . . and impose . . . whereas tactics can only use, manipulate' (30). What interests de

Certeau is the 'multitude of "tactics" articulated in the details of everyday life' (xiv); what he also calls 'poetic ways of "making do" ' (xv). Moreover, 'The tactics of consumption, the ingenious ways in which the weak make use of the strong, thus lend a political dimension to everyday practices' (xvii).

> Many everyday practices (talking, reading, moving about, shopping, cooking, etc.) are tactical in character. And so are, more generally, many 'ways of operating': victories of the 'weak' over the 'strong' (whether the strength be that of powerful people or the violence of things or of an imposed order, etc.), clever tricks, knowing how to get away with things, 'hunter's cunning', manoeuvres. (xix)

Reading a text (he substitutes consumption and production for reading and writing), according to de Certeau has 'all the characteristics of a silent production' as the reader 'insinuates into another person's text the ruses of pleasure and appropriation: he poaches on it' (xxi). In this way, he claims, the reader 'makes the text habitable, like a rented apartment' (ibid.). He describes reading as an ' "art" which is anything but passive', adding that 'the procedures of contemporary consumption appear to constitute a subtle art of "renters" who know how to insinuate their countless differences into the dominant text' (xxii). The cultural critic, therefore, must always be alert to 'the difference or similarity between . . . production . . . and . . . secondary production hidden in the process of . . . utilisation' (xiii). He characterises the active consumption of texts as a form of 'textual poaching', in which 'readers are travellers; they move across lands belonging to someone else, like nomads poaching their way across the fields they did not write' (174).

The acts of textual poaching, or reader appropriation, are always in potential conflict with the 'scriptural economy' (131–76) of textual producers and those institutional voices (professional critics, academics, and so on) who work, through an insistence on the authority of authorial and/or textual meaning, to limit and confine the productive proliferation and circulation of 'unauthorised' meanings. His concept of 'textual poaching' is a rejection of this traditional model of reading, in which the purpose of reading a text is the passive reception of authorial and/or textual intent. It is a model in which reading is reduced to a question of being right or wrong. This model also informs another mode of thinking about consumption, one which assumes that the 'message' of the text is always, in the act of reading, imposed on the reader. De Certeau argues that to assume this is once again to misunderstand the practice of consumption: 'This misunderstanding assumes that "assimilating" necessarily means "becoming similar to" what one absorbs, and not "making something similar" to what one is, making it one's own, appropriating or reappropriating it' (166).

In recent years, fan culture has come increasingly under the critical gaze of cultural studies. One of the most interesting accounts of fan culture from within cultural studies is Henry Jenkins's *Textual Poachers* (1992). Jenkins's principal theoretical source is de Certeau. In an ethnographic investigation of a fan community (mostly, but not exclusively, white middle-class women), Jenkins approaches fan culture as '*both* . . . an academic (who has access to certain theories of popular culture, certain bodies of critical and ethnographic literature) and as a fan (who has access to the particular knowledge and traditions of that community)' (5). The study is written, as Jenkins is quick to point out, 'in active dialogue with the fan community':

> My practice from the outset has been to share each chapter with all of the quoted fans and to encourage their criticism of its contents. I have received numerous letters from fans, offering their own insights into the issues raised here and I have learned much from their reactions. I have met with groups of fans in open discussions of the text and have incorporated their suggestions into its revision. In some cases, I have inserted their reactions into the text, yet, even where this has not occurred directly and explicitly, it must be understood that this text exists in active dialogue with the fan community. (7)

Jenkins's commitment to active dialogue is in part born out of his determination to use his 'institutional authority' to enable him to redefine 'the public identity of fandom', to challenge the negative stereotypes of fans as figures of ridicule or concern, 'and to encourage a greater awareness of the richness of fan culture' (9). The study is written to increase academic knowledge of fan culture, but also with an insistence that academics 'can learn *from* fan culture' (8).

As already noted, acts of reader appropriation are always in potential conflict with the 'scriptural economy', in which reading is reduced to a question of being right or wrong. According to Jenkins:

> What is significant about fans in relation to de Certeau's model is that they constitute a particularly active and vocal community of consumers whose activities direct attention onto this process of cultural appropriation . . . Fans are not unique in their status as textual poachers, yet, they have developed poaching to an art form. (127)

Jenkins differs from de Certeau in that he claims that unlike popular reading, which Jenkins characterises as 'transient meaning-production' (45), fan reading has an ongoing existence in discussions with other fan readers.

> Such discussions expand the experience of the text beyond its initial consumption. The produced meanings are thus more fully integrated into the readers' lives and are of a fundamentally different character from meanings generated through a casual and fleeting encounter with an otherwise unremarkable (and unremarked upon) text. For the fan, these previously 'poached' meanings provide a foundation for future encounters with the fiction, shaping how it will be perceived, defining how it will be used. (45)

A second difference between de Certeau's popular reader and the activities of fandom is that in fandom there is no hard distinction between readers and writers. Fan culture is not just about consumption, it is also about the production of texts – songs, poems, novels, fanzines, videos, etc. – made in response to the professional media texts of fandom. Jenkins (162–77)

151

notes ten ways in which fans rewrite their favourite television shows.

1. *Recontextualisation*: the production of vignettes, short stories and novels which seek to fill in the gaps in broadcast narratives and suggest additional explanations for particular actions.

2. *Expanding the Series Timeline*: the production of vignettes, short stories and novels which provide background history of characters, etc. not explored in broadcast narratives, or suggestions for future developments beyond the period covered by the broadcast narrative.

3. *Refocalisation*: this occurs when fan writers move the focus of attention from the main protagonists to secondary figures. For example, female or black characters are taken from the margins of a text and given centre stage.

4. *Moral Realignment*: a version of refocalisation in which the moral order of the broadcast narrative is inverted (the villains become the good guys). In some versions, the moral order remains the same but the story is now told from the point of view of the villains.

5. *Genre Shifting*: characters from broadcast science-fiction narratives, say, are relocated in the realms of romance or the Western, for example.

6. *Crossovers*: characters from one television programme are introduced into another. For example, characters from *Dr Who* may appear in the same narrative as characters from *Star Wars*.

7. *Character Dislocation*: characters are relocated in new narrative situations, with new names and new identities.

8. *Personalisation*: the insertion of the writer into a version of their favourite television programme. For example, I could write a short story in which I am recruited by the Doctor to travel with him on the TARDIS on a mission to explore what has become of cultural studies in the twenty-fourth century. As Jenkins (171–2) points out, this subgenre of fan writing is discouraged by many in the fan community.

9. *Emotional Intensification*: the production of what are called 'hurt-comfort' stories in which favourite characters, for example, experience emotional crises.

10. *Eroticisation*: stories which explore the erotic side of a character's life. Perhaps the best-known of this subgenre of fan writing is 'slash' fiction, so called because it depicts same-sex relationships (as in Kirk/Spock, Bodie/Doyle, and so on).

In addition to fan fiction, fans make music videos in which images from favourite programmes are edited into new sequences to a soundtrack provided by a popular song; they make fan art; they produce fanzines; they engage in 'filking' (the writing and performing at conferences of songs – filk songs – about programmes, characters or fandom itself); and they organise campaigns (often with some success: see Jenkins 1992, especially Chapter 4) to press television networks to bring back favourite programmes or to make changes in existing ones. As Jenkins points out, 'Fans are poachers who get to keep what they take and use their plundered goods as the foundations for the construction of an alternative cultural community' (223).

According to Jenkins, there are three key features which mark fan culture's mode of appropriation of media texts: '[the] ways fans draw texts close to the realm of their lived experience; the role played by rereading within fan culture; and the process by which program information gets inserted into ongoing social interactions' (53). First of all, then, fan reading is characterised by an intensity of intellectual and emotional involvement.

> The text is drawn close not so that the fan can be possessed by it but rather so that the fan may more fully possess it. Only by integrating media content back into their everyday lives, only by close engagement with its meanings and materials, can fans fully consume the fiction and make it an active resource. (62)

Arguing against textual determinism (the text determines how it will be read and in so doing positions the reader in a particular ideological discourse; see Chapter 4 above), Jenkins insists: 'The reader is drawn not into the preconstituted world of the fiction but rather into a world she has created from textual materials. Here, the reader's pre-established values are at least as important as those preferred by the narrative system'. Again, the difference between fan reader and other readers is a question of the intensity of intellectual and emotional involvement which constitute 'the reader's pre-established values'. The ordinary reader reads in a context of shifting interests; the fan reads from within the realms of the 'lived experience' (63) of fandom.

Second, fans do not just read texts, they continually reread them. This profoundly changes the nature of the text–reader relationship. Roland Barthes (1975) contends that the rereading of texts alters a reader's experience of a text. Rereading undermines the operations of the 'hermeneutic code' (the ways in which a text poses questions to generate the desire to keep reading). Rereading thus shifts the reader's attention from 'what will happen' to 'how things happen', to questions of character relations, narrative themes, the production of social knowledges and discourses.

Finally, whereas most reading is a solitary process, performed in private, fans consume texts as part of a community. Fan culture is about the public display and circulation of meaning production and reading practices. Fans make meanings to communicate with other fans. Without the public display and circulation of these meanings, fandom would not be fandom.

> Organised fandom is, perhaps first and foremost, an institution of theory and criticism, a semistructured space where competing interpretations and evaluations of common texts are proposed, debated, and negotiated and where readers speculate about the nature of the mass media and their own relationship to it. (86)

In his discussion of filking, Jenkins draws attention to a common opposition within filk songs between fandom and 'Mundania' (the world in which non-fans – 'mundane readers' or 'mundanes' – live). The difference between the two worlds is not simply one of intensity of response; 'they are also contrasted in terms of the shallowness and short-sightedness of mundane thinking' (264). 'Fans are defined in opposition to the values and norms of everyday life, as people who live more richly, feel more intensely, play more freely, and think more deeply than "mundanes" ' (268). According to Jenkins, 'Fandom constitutes . . . a space . . . defined by its refusal of mundane values and practices, its celebration of deeply held emotions and passionately embraced pleasures. Fandom's very existence represents a critique of conventional forms of consumer culture' (283).

What Jenkins finds particularly empowering about fandom is its struggle to create 'a more participatory culture' from 'the very forces that transform many Americans into spectators' (284).

> I am not claiming that there is anything particularly empowering about the texts fans embrace. I am, however, claiming that there is something empowering about what fans do with those texts in the process of assimilating them to the particulars of their lives. Fandom celebrates not exceptional texts but rather exceptional readings (though its interpretative practices make it impossible to maintain a clear or precise distinction between the two). (284)

Like the early cultural studies model of subcultural reading, Jenkins's community of fandom is engaged in a struggle to resist the demands of the ordinary and the everyday. Whereas youth subcultures define themselves against parent and dominant cultures, the community of fandom sets itself in opposition to the everyday cultural passivities of 'Mundania'. Lawrence Grossberg (1992) is critical of 'subcultural' models of fandom, in which 'fans constitute an elite fraction of the larger audience of passive consumers' (52).

> Thus, the fan is always in constant conflict, not only with the various structures of power, but also with the vast audience of media consumers. But such an elitist view of fandom does little to illuminate the complex relations that exist between forms of popular culture and their audiences. While we may all agree that there is a difference between the fan and the consumer, we are unlikely to understand the difference if we simply celebrate the former category and dismiss the latter one. (52)

Jenkins's own 'vanguardism' comes, at times, close to this model. Perhaps Fiske (1992b: 46) is right in his assertion that the real difference between a fan and an 'ordinary' reader is 'excess' – the fan is an excessive reader of popular culture.

A key moment in the emergence of shopping as popular culture is the development of the department store in the late nineteenth century. By the close of the nineteenth century the department store had become a familiar feature of city shopping; for example, The Bon Marche in Paris, Harrods in London, Bainbridge in Newcastle-upon-Tyne, Macy's in New York, Wanamaker's in Philadelphia. As Rachel Bowlby explains, 'Within a very short period, department stores had been established as one of the outstanding institutions in the economic and social life of the late nineteenth century; and together with advertising, which was also expanding rapidly, they marked the beginning of present-day consumer society' (1985: 3).

The department store brought into being many of the aspects of shopping we now take for granted. For example, as Bowlby points out:

> The principle of *entrée libre* or open entry did away with what had previously been a moral equation between entering a shop and making a purchase. At the same time, a fixed price policy, supported by clear labelling, put an end to the convention of bargaining which focused attention on shopping as paying. Assistants in department stores received commissions on sales, so were inclined to be flattering rather than argumentative: the customer was now to be waited on rather than negotiated with and money, in appearance, was not part of the exchange (particularly since paying in fact took place in a separate part of the store). People could now come and go, to look and dream, perchance to buy, and shopping became a new bourgeois leisure activity – a way of pleasantly passing the time, like going to a play or visiting a museum. (3–4)

In this way, the discourse of shopping had shifted from an insistence on the 'immediate purchase of particular items' to an attempt to generate and provoke the 'arousal of free-floating desire' (Williams 1982: 67). As Rudi Laermans observes, 'The early department stores pioneered the transformation of traditional customers into modern consumers and of "just merchandise" into spectacular "commodity signs" or "symbolic goods". Thus they laid the cornerstones of a culture we still inhabit' (1993: 94). With this development comes the pleasure of looking, and 'window shopping' and 'just looking' enter for the first time the vocabulary of shopping.[1] But they do not enter everybody's vocabulary: this is a language and an activity for the middle class. Moreover, as Michael B. Miller makes clear, with specific reference to France, but generalisable to other areas of Western Europe and North America, the department store did not simply reflect changing consumer practices, it actively and powerfully contributed to them. 'Far more than a mirror of bourgeois culture in France, the Bon Marché gave shape and defini tion to the very meaning of the concept of a bourgeois way of life' (1981: 182). The department store gave embodiment to this *modus vivendi*; its catalogues operated as a 'cultural primer', telling readers who wanted this way of life, and these specific cultural identities, 'how they should dress, how they should furnish their home, and how they should spent their leisure time' (183). In this way, the department store promoted the idea that a middle-class self was something that could be purchased.

Going shopping is a complex activity. We may visit a shopping centre for a range of different, often contradictory, reasons.[2] We may go to purchase a special gift or to buy the weekly groceries. We may go to look or to be looked at. Shopping centres, as Meaghan Morris (1988) points out, are used by different groups differently:

> [T]here are different practices of use in one centre on any one day: some people may be there for the one and only time in their lives; there are occasional users choosing that centre rather than this on that day for particular, or quite arbitrary reasons; people may shop at one centre and go to another to socialize or hang around. The use of centres as meeting places (and sometimes for free warmth and shelter) by young people, pensioners, the unemployed and the homeless is a

familiar part of their social function – often planned for, now, by centre management (distribution of benches, video games, security guards). (200)

Mike Presdee's (1986) research on the way in which unemployed youths in the South Australian town of Elizabeth use the local shopping centre points to further complexities of consumption. Shopping for the young people of Elizabeth means congregating at the local shopping centre not to buy what is on sale but to consume the public space of the mall. Presdee invents the term 'proletarian shopping' to describe this practice. Young people are not alone in engaging in similar forms of shopping. They are frequently joined by tourists, escapees from bad weather, window shoppers and others who avail themselves of the facilities without necessarily contributing to the profit made by the shopping centre. Fiske (1989b: 18) cites a boutique-owner in an Australian shopping centre who estimated that for every thirty people who visited her shop, only one made a purchase.

Fiske describes shopping centres as 'cathedrals of consumption' (1989b: 13). It is a phrase he immediately regrets, given that it equates consumerism with rituals of profane worship.[3] Fiske is surely right to reject religion as a metaphor for the 'truth' of consumption. Shopping is not a passive ritual of subjugation to the power of consumerism. The 'truth' of consumption is made and remade in the actual act(s) of shopping. Michael Schudson (1984) estimates that in the USA, 90 per cent of new products fail to attract enough consumers to remain in the marketplace. In Australia, John Sinclair (1987) estimates the figure to be about 80 per cent. This is more or less the same failure rate claimed by Simon Frith (1983) with regard to albums and singles in the UK and the USA (see Chapter 6 above). As Fiske points out, 'The power of consumer discrimination evidenced here has no equivalent in the congregation: no religion could tolerate a rejection rate of 80 or 90 per cent of what it has to offer' (1989b: 14).

1. Like most popular pleasures, especially those practised by women, shopping soon attracted its cultural critics. For example, a critic writing in the *New York Times* (June 1881) complained about 'the awful prevalence of the *vice* of shopping among women . . . [an addiction] every bit as bad as male drinking or smoking' (my italics; quoted in Laermans 1993: 88).
2. Shopping centres are about so much more than buying things. Take the example of my local shopping centre, the MetroCentre, Gateshead. It is an attraction in its own right, drawing tourists from around Britain and Europe (especially Scandinavia) to its shops, cinema, bowling alley, restaurants and fairground. Meaghan Morris (1988) gives the example of Indooroopilly Shoppingtown in Queensland, Australia, as 'a place with a postcard' (209).
3. My local shopping centre, Gateshead's MetroCentre, may be a special case: it has its own full-time chaplain.

8

GLOBALISATION AND POPULAR CULTURE

GLOBALISATION

Globalisation refers to the establishment of a capitalist world economy, in which national borders are becoming less and less important as transnational corporations, existing everywhere and nowhere, do business in a global market. This aspect of globalisation can be experienced by simply walking down your 'local' high street, where 'local' goods and services are displayed alongside 'global' goods and services. We encounter the 'global' in the clothes we wear, in the music to which we listen, the television programmes and films we watch, on the internet sites we visit. Perhaps it is most visible when we eat out (or eat in via telephone takeaways). Think, for example, of the culinary pluralism of most British towns and cities, where, say, British fish and chips competes with food which is Indian, East African, Thai, Turkish, Mexican, Chinese, Italian, Spanish, Japanese, and so on. An example of this new culinary pluralism is that Tikka Masala is now regarded as the most popular *British* dish.

Globalisation also refers to what is called 'time-space compression' (Harvey 1990: 240). That is, the way in which the world appears to be getting smaller. 'Shrinking' seems to be occurring in two ways. First, the increased speed and range of travel, together with the fact that more people travel, makes the world seem smaller. Second, the impact of new electronic media on human communications. For example, being near or being distant no longer organises with whom we communicate: electronic media (fax, telephone, email, MSN, Yahoo, Skype) give each of us access to a world well beyond our 'local' community. As a consequence, we may communicate, using, say, email, more with people in Taiwan, Australia, Germany, and the USA, than we do with neighbours who live within 200 metres of where we live. Similarly, television news provides us with images and information about events that are taking place thousands of miles away; unless we watch the 'local' news or read the 'local' newspapers, it is likely that we will be better informed about 'global' events than we are about 'local' events. In this dual sense, then, the 'global' may be more local than the 'local'.

Globalisation also refers to the increasing global mobility of people. It may force workers to travel thousands of miles in search of work. Think of something as everyday as football: over the last few years the English Premier League has featured professional players from many different countries from around the globe.[1] Professional footballers who travel the globe in search of work are certainly the glamorous and wealthy end of labour migrancy, but they are, nevertheless, a sign of a global economy.

GLOBALISATION AS CULTURAL AMERICANISATION

One dominant view of globalisation, especially in discussions of globalisation and popular culture, is to see it as the reduction of the world to an American 'global village': a global village in which everyone speaks English with an American accent, wears Levi jeans and Wrangler shirts, drinks Coca-Cola, eats at McDonalds, surfs the net on a computer overflowing with Microsoft software, listens to rock or country music, watches a mixture of MTV and CNN news broadcasts, Hollywood movies and reruns of *Dallas*, and then discusses the prophetically named World Series, while drinking a bottle of Budweiser or Miller and smoking Marlboro cigarettes. According to this scenario, globalisation is the successful global imposition of American culture, in which the economic success of

US capitalism is underpinned by the cultural work that its commodities supposedly do in effectively destroying indigenous cultures and imposing an American way of life on 'local' populations. There are at least four problems with this view of globalisation.

The first problem with a model of globalisation as cultural Americanisation is that it assumes that 'economic' success is the same as cultural imposition. In other words, the recognition of the obvious success of US companies in placing products in most of the markets of the world is understood as self-evidently and unproblematically 'cultural' success. Success in the economic sphere equals success in the cultural sphere; in this way, the cultural is flattened into the economic, as if it were nothing more than a manifestation of an always reliable effect. For example, American sociologist Herbert Schiller (1979), claims that the ability of American companies successfully to unload commodities around the globe is producing an American global capitalist culture. The role of media corporations, he claims, is to make programmes which 'provide in their imagery and messagery, the beliefs and perspectives that create and reinforce their audiences' attachments to the way things are in the system overall' (30).

There are two overlapping problems with Schiller's position. First, it is simply assumed that commodities are the same as culture; establish the presence of the former and you can predict the details of the latter. But as John Tomlinson (1999) points out, '[I]f we assume that the sheer global presence of these goods is *in itself* token of a convergence towards a capitalist monoculture, we are probably utilising a rather impoverished concept of culture – one that reduces culture to its material goods' (83). It may be the case that certain commodities are used, made meaningful and valued in ways which promote capitalism as a way of life, but this is not something which can be established by simply assuming that market penetration is the same as ideological penetration.

This is not to deny that American capitalism is working – selling goods, making profits – but it is to deny that its success is the result of people being too stupid to realise that if they drink Coca-Cola or wear Levi jeans their indigenous culture will be destroyed and they will become Americanised.

The second problem with Schiller's position is that it is an argument which depends on the claim that commodities have inherent values and singular meanings, which can be imposed on passive consumers. In other words, his argument operates with a very discredited account of the flow of influence. It simply assumes that the dominant globalising culture will be successfully injected into the weaker 'local' culture. That is, it is assumed that people are the passive consumers of the cultural meanings which supposedly flow directly and straightforwardly from the commodities they consume. We should recall here de Certeau's point about a general misunderstanding of the practice of consumption: 'This misunderstanding assumes that "assimilating" necessarily means "becoming similar to" what one absorbs, and not "making something similar" to what one is, making it one's own, appropriating or reappropriating it' (166).

In *The Export of Meaning*, Tamar Liebes and Elihu Katz (1993) investigated the international consumption of *Dallas* (watched in over ninety countries in the early 1980s). The question they sought to answer was whether or not American television programmes like *Dallas* are anything more than just cultural commodities for sale in the global marketplace, 'but also agents [for the] subversion of indigenous values' (1993: viii). To fathom the cultural and political influence of *Dallas*, they studied the reception of the serial in three national contexts: Israel, America, and Japan. In Israel they studied four groups: veteran kibbutz members of Western origin, new immigrants from Russia, Israeli Arabs, and Moroccan Jews. For further comparison, they included in their sample American viewers in Los Angeles, part of the programme's original audience, and Japanese viewers in Tokyo, one of the few places where *Dallas* failed.

When asked to retell an episode from *Dallas*:

> some groups chose to represent the story more sociologically, as if it were the story of a linear progress through a social obstacle course. Other groups retold the story more psychologically, emphasising the motivations and personalities of the characters, while yet others retold the story in terms of themes and leitmotifs. (152)

When questioned about particular details in the narrative of an episode, some groups (for example, Moroccan Jews and Israeli Arabs) employed a referential frame (reading the programme in relation to their own lives) to explain what had happened in terms of 'real life'. Other groups, the American and kibbutz groups, for example, used a critical frame (reading the text as text) and explained what had happened in terms of genre.

One significant difference between the groups concerned the framing discourse chosen to interpret the programme. For the Americans, kibbutzniks and Japanese, the framing discourse was aesthetic; for the Moroccan Jews it was moral; and for the Russians immigrants it was ideological. For example, one Russian respondent described *Dallas* as 'propaganda for the American way of life' (76). On the other hand, an Israeli Arab condemned in more general terms the life the programme supposedly depicts, 'When materialism dominates, society falls apart, and the material begins to be everything' (88). One Japanese viewer had difficulty taking the programme seriously because of the way in which it violated his sense of social realism, '[I]t is hard to believe that such a marriage between Bobby and the girl, which is typical to the middle class, happens in high society' (134).

The conclusion Liebes and Katz draw from their study is that a programmes like *Dallas* 'may beam a homogeneous message to the global village, but our study argues that there is pluralism in the decoding' (152). In other words, although the different groups offered distinct ways in which to understand *Dallas*, they can all clearly be seen to relate to the 'content' of the programme – the programme is the same for all the groups; what is different, and inflects how *Dallas* is understood, is the cultural mode of understanding that each group brings to their involvement with it.

A second problem with globalisation as cultural Americanisation is that it operates with a limited concept of the 'foreign'. First of all, it works with the assumption that what is foreign is always a question of national difference. But what is foreign can equally be a question of class, ethnicity, gender, sexuality, generation, or any other marker of social difference (see Figure 4). Moreover, what is foreign in terms of being imported from another country may be less foreign than differences already established by, say, class or generation. Furthermore, the imported foreign may be used against the prevailing power relations of the 'local'. This is probably what is happening with the export of 'hip hop'. What are we to make of the global success of hip hop? Are South African, French or British rappers (and fans of hip hop) the victims of American cultural imperialism? Are they the cultural dupes of a transnational music industry? A more interesting approach would be to look at how South Africans, French or British youth have 'appropriated' hip hop; used it to meet their local needs and desires. In other words, the approach would be one which looked at what they do with it, rather than only what it supposedly does to them. American culture is worked on; it is used to make space within what is perceived as the dominant national culture.

The 'Foreign'

national	class
	ethnicity
	gender
	generation
	'race'
	sexuality

Figure 4

Another problem with this very limited notion of the foreign is that it is always assumed that the 'local' is the same as the national. But within the national there may well be many 'locals'. Moreover, there may be considerable conflict between them and between them and the dominant culture (that is, 'the national'). As Annabelle Sreberny-Mohammadi (1991) explains:

> National agendas are not coincidental with truly 'local' agendas, and real concerns arise as to whether 'national' media cultures adequately represent ethnic, religious, political and other kinds of diversity. In international relations, the

'national' is itself a site of struggle, with a variety of "local" identities and voices in contention. (Sreberny-Mohammadi 1991: 129)

Globalisation can therefore both help confirm or help undo local cultures; it can keep one in place and it can make one suddenly feel out of place. For example, in 1946, addressing a conference of Spanish clerics, the Archbishop of Toledo wondered 'how to tackle', what he called:

> women's growing demoralization – caused largely by American customs introduced by the cinematograph, making the young woman independent, breaking up the family, disabling and discrediting the future consort and mother with exotic practices that make her less womanly and destabilize the home. (quoted in Tomlinson 1997: 123)

Spanish women may have taken a different view.

Globalisation is much more complex and contradictory than the simple imposition of, say, American culture. Now it is certainly true that we can travel around the world while never being too far from signs of American commodities. What is not true, however, is that commodities equal culture. Globalisation involves the ebb and flow of both homogenising and heterogenising forces; the meeting and the mingling of the 'local' and the 'global'. Roland Robertson (1995) uses the term 'glocalization' (borrowed from the language of Japanese business) to describe globalisation as the simultaneous interpenetration of the 'global' and the 'local'. To understand this in a different way, what is exported always finds itself in the context of what already exists. That is, exports become imports, as they are incorporated into the indigenous culture. This can in turn impact on the cultural production of the 'local'. Ien Ang (1996) gives the example of the Cantonese Kung Fu movies which revitalised the declining Hong Kong film industry. The films are a mixture of 'western' narratives and Cantonese values. As she explains:

> Culturally speaking, it is hard to distinguish here between the 'foreign' and the 'indigenous', the 'imperialist' and the

'authentic': what has emerged is a highly distinctive and economically viable hybrid cultural form in which the global and the local are inextricably intertwined, in turn leading to the modernized reinvigoration of a culture that continues to be labelled and widely experienced as 'Cantonese'. In other words, what counts as 'local' and therefore 'authentic' is not a fixed content, but subject to change and modification as a result of the domestication of imported cultural goods. (154–5)

The processes of globalisation may be making the world smaller, generating new forms of cultural hybridity, but it is also bringing into collision and conflict different ways of making the world mean. While some people may celebrate the opening up of new global 'routes', other people may resist globalisation in the name of local 'roots'. Resistance in the form of a reassertion of the local against the flow of the global can be seen in the increase in religious fundamentalism (Christianity, Hinduism, Islam, and Judaism) and the re-emergence of nationalism, most recently in the former Soviet Union and the former Yugoslavia. A more benign example of the insistence on 'roots' is the explosive growth in family history research in Europe and the USA. In all of these examples, globalisation may be driving the search for 'roots' in a more secure past in the hope of stabilising identities in the present.

A third problem with globalisation as cultural Americanisation is that it assumes that America is the only global power. But the world is made up of many changing centres of power. The global economic status of China, South Korea, Singapore, and especially Japan, should certainly problematise any straightforward idea of globalisation as Americanisation. With the rise of these other global economies cultural flows can no longer be understood as moving from the American imperial centre to the colonial periphery. As David Morley (1996) observes, '[M]odernity (or perhaps postmodernity) may perhaps in future, be located more in the Pacific than the Atlantic' (349). Although this means that globalisation may lack an obvious centre, it is still marked by what Doreen Massey (1994) calls 'power geometry' (149): some people travel, some do not; and some travel because they are forced to move in search of work or away from political repression. Similarly, some people have the power to make things happen, while others seem to be always those to whom things happen, their lives continually shaped and structured by the powerful actions of unknown people from a distant elsewhere.

Massey also makes the very perceptive point that many of the anxieties revealed in 'Western' discussions of globalisation may represent a particular understanding of the world: a view from the West, unconsciously nostalgic for the simpler times of colonialism. As she explains:

> The sense of dislocation which some feel at the sight of a once well-known local street now lined by a succession of cultural imports – the pizzeria, the kebab house, the branch of the middle-eastern bank – must have been felt for centuries . . . by colonized peoples all over the world. (147)

This would have been the experience of people as they witnessed first, the importation of British, and then American, institutions and commodities. She complains, quite rightly I think, about the fact that much of this writing on globalisation is written 'from the point of view of a (relative) elite. Those who today worry about a sense of disorientation and a loss of control must once have felt they knew exactly where they were, and that they *had* control' (165). In other words, to see the penetration of the boundaries of the 'local' as something of recent origin is to read history from the perspective of a colonising First World:

> For the security of the boundaries of the place one called home must have dissolved long ago, and the coherence of one's local culture must long ago have been under threat, in those parts of the world where the majority of its population lives. In those parts of the world, it is centuries now since time and distance provided much protective insulation from the outside. (165–6)

The fourth problem with the model of globalisation as cultural Americanisation is that it assumes that American culture is mono-lithic. Even in the more guarded accounts of globalisation it is assumed that we can identify something singular called American culture. George Ritzer (1999), for example, makes this claim, '[W] hile we will continue to see global diversity, many, most, perhaps eventually all of those cultures will be affected by American exports: America will become virtually everyone's "second culture" ' (89). Globalisation as cultural Americanisation assumes that cultures can be lined up as distinct monolithic entities, hermetically sealed from one another until the fatal moment of the globalising injection. Against such a view, Jan Nederveen Pieterse (1995) argues that globalisation is better understood 'as a process of hybridization which gives rise to a global mélange' (45). He points to 'phenomena such as Thai boxing by Moroccan girls in Amsterdam, Asian rap in London, Irish bagels, Chinese tacos and Mardi Gras Indians in the United States, or Mexican schoolgirls dressed in Greek togas dancing in the style of Isidora Duncan' (53). To see globalisation as simply a process of the export of sameness is to miss so much of what is going on.

> It [globalisation as homogenisation] overlooks the counter-currents – the impact non-Western cultures have been making on the West. It downplays the ambivalence of the globalising momentum and ignores the role of local reception of Western culture – for example the indigenization of Western elements. It fails to see the influence non-Western cultures have been exercising on one another. It has no room for crossover culture – as in the development of "third cultures" such as world music. It overrates the homogeneity of Western culture and overlooks the fact that many of the standards exported by the West and its cultural industries themselves turn out to be of culturally mixed character if we examine their cultural lineages. (ibid.)

Moreover, the idea of globalisation as the imposition of a singular and monolithic American culture begins to look very different when we consider the fact that the United States has the third largest Hispanic population in the world. Also, it is estimated that by 2076, the tricentennial of the American Revolution, that people of Native American, African, Asian or Latin descent, will make up the majority of its population. Stuart Hall (1996b) has written that postmodernism 'is about how the world dreams itself to be American' (132).

If this is the case, we are all dreaming of many different Americas, depending on which bits of America we choose to consume. For example, if the material for our dreams is gathered from American popular music, the geography and geometry, the values, images, myths, styles, will be different depending on whether, for example, it is blues, country, dance, folk, heavy metal, jazz, rap, rock'n'roll, sixties rock, or soul. At the very least, each genre of music would produce different political articulations, in terms of class, gender, race, ethnicity, sexuality, generation. To recognise this is to recognise that cultures, even powerful cultures like that of the United States, are never monolithic. As Edward Said (1993) observes, '[A]ll cultures are involved in one another; none is single and pure, all are hybrid, heterogeneous, extraordinarily differentiated, and unmonolithic' (xxix). Moreover:

> No one today is purely one thing. Labels like Indian, or woman, or Muslim, or American are now [no] more than starting points, which if followed into actual experience for only a moment are quickly left behind. Imperialism consolidated the mixture of cultures and identities on a global scale. But its worst and most paradoxical gift was to allow people to believe that they were only, mainly exclusively, White, or Black, or Western, or Oriental. (407–8)

Annabelle Sreberny-Mohammadi (1991), commenting on Jeremy Tunstall's *The Media Are American* (1978), in which he worries responsibly about how the imposition of American culture will destroy authentic indigenous culture or at least produce hybrid concoctions, says:

> But we must ask what is the pristine image of culture that lurks behind this argument? Human history is a history of cultural contact, influence and recombination, as is evidenced in language, music, visual arts, philosophical systems; perhaps media flows merely reinforce our mongrel statuses. (129)

However, to celebrate hybridity and to forget about global power relations would be to miss even more than those who see globalisation as cultural Americanisation; cultural hybridity is not without its relations of power. As Nederveen Pieterse (1995) observes, 'Hybridity raises the question of the *terms* of mixture, the conditions of mixing' (57). But, as he also observes, 'Cultures have been hybrid *all along*, hybridization is in effect a tautology: contemporary accelerated globalisation means the hybridization of hybrid cultures' (64). He argues, 'Hybridity unsettles the introverted [territorial] concept of culture which underlies romantic nationalism, racism, ethnicism, religious revivalism, civilizational chauvinism, and culturalist essentialism' (ibid.).

> In relation to the global human condition of inequality, the hybridization perspective releases reflection and engagement from the boundaries of nation, community, ethnicity, or class. Fixities have become fragments as the kaleidoscope of collective experience is in motion. It has been in motion all along and the fixities of nation, community, ethnicity and class have been grids superimposed upon experiences more complex and subtle than reflexivity and organization could accommodate. (ibid.)

HEGEMONY AND GLOBALISATION

Globalisation is a complex process, producing contradictory effects, in changing relations of culture and power. One way to understand the processes of globalisation is in terms of the cultural studies appropriation of Gramsci's concept of hegemony. As we noted in Chapter 1, according to cultural studies informed by hegemony theory, popular culture is neither an 'authentic' subordinate culture, nor a culture imposed by the culture industries, but a 'compromise equilibrium' (Gramsci) between the two; a contradictory mix of forces from both 'below' and 'above'; both 'commercial' and 'authentic'; marked by 'resistance' and 'incorporation', involving both 'structure' and 'agency'. Globalisation can also be seen in this way. As Hall observes:

> [W]hat we usually call the global, far from being something which, in a systematic fashion, rolls over everything, creating similarity, in fact works through particularity, negotiates

171

particular spaces, particular ethnicities, works through mobilizing particular identities and so on. So there is always a dialectic, between the local and the global. (Hall 1991: 62)

Like globalisation hegemony is a complex and contradictory process; it is not the same as injecting people with 'false consciousness'. It is certainly not explained by the adoption of the assumption that 'hegemony is prepackaged in Los Angeles, shipped out to the global village, and unwrapped in innocent minds' (Liebes and Katz 1993: xi). A better way to understand the processes of globalisation is one which takes seriously, not just the power of global forces but also those of the local. This is not to deny power but to insist that a politics in which ordinary people are seen as mute and passive victims of a process they can never hope to understand, a politics which denies agency to the vast majority or at best only recognises certain activities as signs of agency, is a politics which can exist without causing too much trouble to the prevailing structures of global power. We must always keep in play the dialogue of structure and agency. As Marx famously described it:

> Men make their own history, but they do not make it just as they please; they do not make it under circumstances chosen by themselves, but under circumstances directly encountered, given and transmitted from the past. (1977: 10)

We make culture and we are made by culture.

NOTE

1. Since the 1990s the English Premier League has featured professional players from around the globe, including from: Algeria, Argentina, Australia, Austria, Belgium, Bermuda, Bosnia, Brazil, Bulgaria, Cameroon, Canada, Chile, Columbia, Congo, Costa Rica, Croatia, Czech Republic, Denmark, Eire, Ecuador, Estonia, Finland, France, Germany, Greece, Holland, Iceland, Israel, Italy, Jamaica, Japan, Latvia, Liberia, Morocco, Nigeria, Northern Ireland, Norway, Peru, Poland, Portugal, Russia, Scotland, South Africa, Spain, Sweden, Switzerland, Trinidad, Turkey, Ukraine, Uruguay, United States, Venezuela, Wales, and Yugoslavia.

9

POSTSCRIPT: THE CIRCUIT OF CULTURE

Cultural studies, as we noted in Chapter 1, insists that the meaning of something always depends on context. Moreover, rather than simply insist that context is important, it insists on multiple contexts, knowing that an object of study will look very different in different contexts. Cultural studies has attempted to think this idea in different ways, but one recent, and very useful, approach is the circuit of culture (see Figure 5) as developed by Paul du Gay and others at the Open University (du Gay el al., 1997). According to this model, there are five interrelated contexts we must consider if we are to fully understand a text or practice: representation, identity, production, consumption and regulation. At each point in the circuit an object of study will seem different. But to repeat, these are not independent contexts but interrelated. Therefore, a fully adequate analysis must always take into account each in turn while recognising that each will be entangled with other moments in the circuit. To demonstrate this I will briefly take the Manchester United football shirt around the circuit.

Although we can start at any point on the circuit, I will begin with representation. How is the Manchester United shirt represented? How are its meanings discursively constructed? What kinds of meanings do the advertisers seek to encode into the shirt. A great deal of the promotional material shows images of United's players,

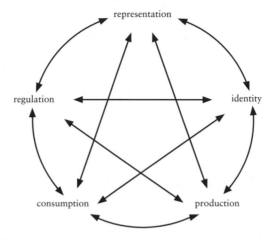

The circuit of culture

Figure 5

past and present, in action, usually in celebratory mode (after a goal or lifting a trophy). The suggestion here is clear: buy the shirt (or several of the different ones on offer) and become part of the Manchester United tradition. The website *Pride of Manchester* is very explicit about the relationship between tradition and owning a Manchester United shirt.

> Pride Of Manchester bring you the most comprehensive history of Manchester United kits, with details of every jersey ever worn, many of which you can still buy online. From Newton Heath's lace up green and yellow strip, to the brand new AIG-sponsored Nike Manchester United shirt for the 2009–10 season, we've got images of nearly every Man United shirt ever worn . . . Enjoy browsing as we take you back on a nostalgic journey. (http://www.prideofmanchester. com/sport/mufc-kits.htm)

If we remove the final clause of the first sentence, we might think we are reading a museum catalogue, rather than the promotional material of a website selling Manchester United shirts. At the moment of representation the Manchester United shirt is a site for the production of dreams of belonging and the associated glories that supposedly come with wearing the shirt. Considered from this point on the circuit the meaning of the shirt is clear: it is a commodity that markets itself as an opportunity to become a part of glories past and present. The shirt is offered as a visual sign of membership to a tradition and a global fan community.

Considering the shirt in terms of production raises questions regarding the manufacture of the shirt. Over recent years there has been a growing awareness of the often appalling labour conditions in which clothing for Western markets, including football shirts, are manufactured. In June 2009 the *News of the World* reported that children in Indonesia were being paid 16p an hour to make England football shirts that sold for £49 (http://www.newsoftheworld.co.uk/news/358888/Sweat-shop-labourers-paid-just-pound2-a-day-to-churn-out-pound49-England-football-kit.html). The sportswear consultant and designer Susan Acton estimated in 1997 that replica shirts, mostly made in the Far East, cost around £5 to make and are sold to sportswear companies for around £7.50, and are then sold to retailers, like the Manchester United Superstore, for around £13.50, to go on sale to the public for around £35 (http://findarticles.com/p/articles/mi_qn4161/is_19970518/ai_n14463980/).

Football shirts are certainly an enormous source of income. Manchester United are paid by Nike for the licence to make their shirts (in 2000 the club signed a £302.9 million sponsorship and merchandising deal with Nike). The club then sells space on the shirt to a sponsor. In June 2009 Manchester United signed a sponsorship deal with the Aon Corporation (a US financial company), which agreed to pay the club £20 million a year for its logo to appear on United's shirt from the 2010/11 season. As Greg Case, president and chief executive officer of Aon, explains, 'Manchester United has one of the most recognised sports brands in the world. [They] are all about winning and about excellence; the same holds true for the Aon team' (http://www.uksponsorship.com/jun09manu.htm). From the perspective of Aon, the shirt is a site to help build its brand by being associated with a successful global brand. Tradition and glories, past and present, are now a means to make money.

What can we say about the shirt in terms of identity and identity formation? The most obvious thing to point to is that wearing the shirt is to identify, and be identified, as a supporter of Manchester United. The branding strategies of Aon are largely irrelevant to this process. It is now very common to see people on holiday wearing football shirts, identifying both who they support and, in most cases, the towns or cities in which they live. We can see these mobile communities forming and reforming on beaches and in bars in places like Greece, Turkey and Spain. One very moving sign of the link between identity and football shirts is the way shirts are often used as a part of roadside shrines at the sites of fatal accidents. Here the shirt is standing in for the lost loved one; embodying a key aspect of their identity. This meaning of the shirt is a long way from the meaning it has for Aon or Nike and their global branding strategies.

Questions of identity obviously connect to questions of consumption. Most football clubs have a shop or superstore where fans can buy all manner of items connected to the team they support. Manchester United has a superstore that sells everything from footballs, kits, books, mugs, to baby clothes, wallpaper, jewellery and fashion items. Consumption in these stores is driven by a desire to connect emotionally with the team and is clearly a fundamental aspect of the processes of identifying with the club one supports. We use consumption to transform our social worlds, including the making and remaking of our identities. Therefore, as we discussed in Chapter 7, the meaning of the shirt for Manchester United fans is not determined by its production but by how it is consumed. So what it means to Nike, Aon or Manchester United does not determine what it means for the fans who buy the shirts. In simple terms, there is a difference between the shirt as a site for the making of profit and the shirt as a visual sign in the making and remaking of fan identities. To really understand what fans make in their acts of consumption requires that we engage in ethnographic research. Such meanings cannot be read off from how the shirt is produced and represented.

Finally, what can we say about the shirt in terms of regulation? There are two points we might make here. First, there has been a great deal of concern that clubs exploit their fans by producing an unnecessary number of expensive shirts for fans to buy. According to a report in 2002, 'Shirts are now the largest earner for clubs in a replica kit market worth an estimated £250m a year' (http://www.independent.co.uk/news/business/news/whistle-blown-on-pricefixing-of-replica-shirts-651433.html). As we have seen already, the difference between the cost of making the shirt and price it sells for is enormous. In March 1998, Freddy Shepherd and Douglas Hall, then directors of Newcastle United, were caught on video by the *News of the World* mocking their club's own supporters for paying extortionate amounts of money for football shirts. In 2003 the UK Office of Fair Trading fined Manchester United £1.5 million for its involvement with sportswear companies in fixing the price of football shirts. These media stories, and the general sense that the gap between cost and profit is excessive, have led to many calls for government to regulate the sale of football shirts (that is, reduce the price and the frequency with which clubs change their shirts). A second form of regulation is much more informal and seeks to 'regulate' when and where we wear a football shirt. Obviously there are social occasions when the wearing of a football shirt seems totally inappropriate – events, for example, that require a formal dress code. But there are also places where a Manchester United supporter would not wear the shirt. For instance, it would be a little foolish to wear it in certain pubs in Liverpool on days when Liverpool are playing at home.

In each of these moments in the circuit the Manchester United shirt signifies something different. At the point of representation we see a collision of production and consumption, as production is prepared for consumption. In terms of identity the shirt is the most visible sign of one's membership of the Manchester United global fan community. Explored in terms of production the shirt is a commodity, a site for the generation of capital. At the same point it is also a symbol of the often exploitative relations between East and West. It is at the moment of consumption that fans produce and reproduce in visible circulation the culture of Manchester United. Addressing the shirt at the point of regulation, the shirt becomes something to control: its price and when and where it is right to wear it. But, as we noted earlier, there is often a certain overlap between what the shirt means in two or more parts of the circuit. However, taking the shirt around the circuit provides us with a fuller, more adequate, understanding of the contemporary meanings of the Manchester United football shirt. To analyse the shirt, or anything else, from only one point in the circuit would be to miss a great deal that is significant and of interest, producing an analysis that would seriously misrepresent the object of study.

REFERENCES

Adorno, T. W. (2009) 'On Popular Music'. In J. Storey (ed.), *Cultural Theory and Popular Culture: A Reader*, 4th edn, London: Pearson, 63–74.

Allen, (ed.) (1992) *Channels of Discourse, Reassembled*, London: Routledge.

Althusser, L. (1969) *For Marx*, Harmondsworth: Penguin.

Althusser, L. (1971) *Lenin and Philosophy*, New York: Monthly Review Press.

Althusser, L. and Balibar, E. (1979) *Reading Capital*, London: Verso.

Althusser, L. (2009) 'Ideology and Ideological State Apparatuses'. In J. Storey (ed.), *Cultural Theory and Popular Culture: A Reader*, 4th edn, London: Pearson, 302–12.

Ang, I. (1985) *Watching Dallas*, London: Methuen.

Ang, I. (1989) 'Wanted: Audience'. In E. Seiter, H. Borchers, G. Kreutzner, E. M. Warth (eds), *Remote Control*, London: Routledge.

Ang, I. (1991) *Watching Television*, London: Routledge.

Ang, I. (1996) 'Culture and Communication: Towards an Ethnographic Critique of Media Consumption in the Transnational Media System'. In J. Storey (ed.), *What is Cultural Studies?: A Reader*, London: Edward Arnold, 237–54.

Ang, I. (2009) 'Feminist Desire and Female Pleasure'. In J. Storey (ed.), *Cultural Theory and Popular Culture: A Reader*, 4th edn, London: Pearson, 581–90.

Appleby, J. (1993) 'A Different Kind of Independence: The Post-war Restructuring of the Historical Study of Early America', *William and Mary Quarterly* 50: 245–67.

Arnold, M. (2009) 'Culture and Anarchy'. In J. Storey (ed.), *Cultural*

Theory and Popular Culture: A Reader, 4th edn, London: Pearson, 6–11.

Barthes, R. (1967) *Elements of Semiology*, London: Jonathan Cape.

Barthes, R. (1973) 'Preface'. In *Mythologies*, London: Jonathan Cape, 11–12.

Barthes, R. (1975) *The Pleasure of the Text*, New York: Hill and Wang.

Barthes, R. (1977a) 'The Photographic Message'. In *Image – Music – Text*, London: Routledge, 15–31.

Barthes, R. (1977b) 'The Grain of the Voice'. In *Image – Music – Text*, London: Routledge, 179–89.

Barthes, R. (2009) 'Myth Today'. In J. Storey (ed.), *Cultural Theory and Popular Culture: A Reader*, 4th edn, London: Pearson, 261–9.

Bausinger, H. (1984) 'Media, Technology and Everyday Life'. In *Media, Culture and Society* 6: 4, 343–51.

Bermingham, A. (1995) 'The Consumption of Culture: Image, Object, Text'. In A. Bermingham and J. Brewer (eds) (1995) *The Consumption of Culture 1600–1800: Image, Object, Text*, London: Routledge, 1–20.

Bennett, T. and Woollacott, J. (1987) *Bond and Beyond*, London: Macmillan.

Bowlby, R. (1985) *Just Looking: Consumer Culture in Dreiser, Gissing and Zola*, London: Methuen.

Brooks, P. (1976) *The Melodramatic Imagination*, New Haven, NY: Yale University Press.

Brown, M. E. (1990) 'Motley Moments: Soap Opera, Carnival, Gossip and the Power of the Utterance'. In M. E. Brown (ed.), *Television and Women's Culture: The Politics of the Popular*, London: Sage Publications, 96–126.

Brunsdon, C. (1991) 'Pedagogies of the Feminine: Feminist Teaching and Women's Genres', *Screen* 32: 4, 364–81.

Brunsdon, C. and Morley, D. (1978) *Everyday Television: 'Nationwide'*, London: British Film Institute.

Burgess, J. and Green, J. (2009) *YouTube: Online Video and Participatory Culture*, Cambridge: Polity Press.

Carter, E. (1984) 'Alice in the Consumer Wonderland: West German Case Studies in Gender and Consumer Culture'. In A. McRobbie and M. Nava (eds), *Gender and Generation*, London: Macmillan, 185–214.

Certeau, M. de (1984) *The Practice of Everyday Life*, Berkeley, CA: University of California Press.

Chambers, I. (1985) *Urban Rhythms: Pop Music and Popular Culture*, London: Macmillan.

Chodorow, N. (1978) *The Reproduction of Mothering*, Berkeley, CA: University of California Press.

Clarke, G. (1990) 'Defending Ski-jumpers: A Critique of Theories of Youth Subcultures'. In S. Frith and A. Goodwin (eds), *On Record: Rock, Pop and the Written Word*, New York: Pantheon, 81–96.

Clarke, J., Hall, S., Jefferson, T. and Roberts, B. (1976) 'Subcultures,

References

Culture and Class'. In S. Hall and T. Jefferson (eds), *Resistance through Rituals*, London: Hutchinson, 9–74.

Cohen, P. (1980) 'Subcultural Conflict and Working-class Community'. In S. Hall, D. Hobson, A. Lowe and P. Willis (eds), *Culture, Media, Language*, London: Hutchinson, 78–87.

Connell, I. (1992) 'Personalities in the Popular Media'. In P. Dahlgren and C. Sparks (eds), *Journalism and Popular Culture*, London: Sage, 64–83.

Coward, R. (1984) *Female Desire*, London: Paladin.

Cruz, J. and Lewis, J. (eds) (1994) *Viewing, Reading, Listening*, Boulder, CO: Westview Press.

Dahlgren, P. (1992) 'Introduction'. In P. Dahlgren and C. Sparks (eds), *Journalism and Popular Culture*, London: Sage, 1–23.

Denselow, R. (1989) *When the Music's Over: The Story of Political Pop*, London: Faber and Faber.

Du Gay, P., Hall, S., James, L., Mackay, H., and Negus, K. (1997) *Doing Cultural Studies: The Story of the Sony Walkman*, London: Sage.

Dyer, R. (1977) 'Victim: Hermeneutic Project', *Film Form* 1: 2, 1–10.

Dyer, R. (1981) 'Entertainment and Utopia'. In R. Altman (ed.), *Genre: The Musical: A Reader*, London: Routledge & Kegan Paul, 175–89.

Fish, S. (1980) *Is there a Text in this Class? The Authority of Interpretative Communities*, Cambridge, MA: Harvard University Press.

Fisher, J. (1989c) 'Moments of Television: Neither the Text nor the Audience'. In E. Seiter, H. Borchers, G. Kreutzner, E. M. Warth (eds), *Remote Control*, London: Routledge, 56–78.

Fiske, J. (1987) *Television Culture*, New York: Routledge.

Fiske, J. (1989a) *Understanding Popular Culture*, Boston, MA: Unwin Hyman.

Fiske, J. (1989b) *Reading Popular Culture*, Boston, MA: Unwin Hyman.

Fiske, J. (1992a) 'Popularity and the Politics of Information'. In P. Dahlgren and C. Sparks (eds), *Journalism and Popular Culture*, London: Sage, 43–63.

Fiske, J. (1992b) 'The Cultural Economy of Fandom'. In L. Lewis (ed.), *The Adoring Audience: Fan Culture and Popular Media*, London: Routledge, 30–49.

Foucault, M. (1972) *The Archaeology of Knowledge*, London: Tavistock.

Foucault, M. (1979) *Discipline and Punish*, Harmondsworth: Penguin.

Foucault, M. (2001a) 'Questions of Method'. In *Essential Works of Michel Foucault*, vol. 3: Power, J. D. Faubion (eds), Harmondsworth: Penguin, 223–38.

Foucault, M. (2001b), 'The Subject and Power'. In *Essential Works of Michel Foucault*, vol. 3: Power, J. D. Faubion (eds), Harmondsworth: Penguin, 326–48.

Freud, S. (1986) *The Interpretation of Dreams*, Harmondsworth: Penguin.

Frith, S. (1983) *Sound Effects*, London: Constable.

Frith, S. and McRobbie, A. (1990) 'Rock and Sexuality'. In S. Frith and A. Goodwin (eds), *On Record: Rock, Pop and the Written Word*, London: Routledge, 371–89.

Frow, J. and Morris, M. (1996) 'Australian Cultural Studies'. In J. Storey (ed.), *What is Cultural Studies?: A Reader*, London: Edward Arnold, 344–67.

Gadamer, H.-G. (1979) *Truth and Method*, London: Sheed and Ward.

Gamman, L. and Marshment, L. (eds) (1988) *The Female Gaze: Women as Viewers of Popular Culture*, London: Verso.

Gledhill, C. (2009) 'Pleasurable Negotiations'. In J. Storey (ed.), *Cultural Theory and Popular Culture: A Reader*, 4th edn, London: Pearson, 98–110.

Golding, P. and Murdock, G. (1991) 'Culture, Communications and Political Economy'. In J. Curran and M. Gurevitch (eds), *Mass Media and Society*, London: Edward Arnold, 15–32.

Gramsci, A. (1971) *Selections from Prison Notebooks*, London: Lawrence and Wishart.

Gramsci, A. (2009) 'Hegemony, Intellectuals and the State'. In J. Storey (ed.), *Cultural Theory and Popular Culture: A Reader*, 4th edn, London: Pearson, 75–80.

Gripsrud, J. (1992) 'The Aesthetics and Politics of Melodrama'. In P. Dahlgren and C. Sparks (eds), *Journalism and Popular Culture*, London: Sage.

Grossberg, L. (1983) 'Cultural Studies Revisited'. In M. Mander (ed.), *Communications in Transition*, New York: Praeger, 39–70.

Grossberg, L. (1992) 'Is there a Fan in the House?: The Affective Sensibility of Fandom'. In L. Lewis (ed.), *The Adoring Audience: Fan Culture and Popular Media*, London: Routledge, 50–65.

Hall, S. (1980) 'Encoding and Decoding in the Television Discourse'. In S. Hall, D. Hobson, A. Lowe and P. Willis (eds), *Culture, Media, Language*, London: Hutchinson, 128–38.

Hall, S. (1991) 'Old and New Ethnicities'. In A. Smith (ed.), *Culture, Globalization and the World-System*, London: Macmillan.

Hall, S. (1992) 'Cultural Studies and its Theoretical Legacies'. In L. Grossberg, C. Nelson and P. Treichler (eds), *Cultural Studies*, London: Routledge, 277–94.

Hall, S. (1996a) 'Cultural Studies: Two Paradigms'. In J. Storey (ed.), *What is Cultural Studies?: A Reader*, London: Arnold, 31–48.

Hall, S. (1996b) 'On Postmodernism and Articulation'. In D. Morley and K.-H. Chen (eds), *Stuart Hall: Critical Dialogues in Cultural Studies*, London: Routledge, 131–50.

Hall, S. (1997) 'The Work of Representation'. In Stuart Hall (ed.), *Representation: Cultural Representations and Signifying Practices*, London: Sage, 15–64.

Hall, S. (2009) 'Notes on Deconstructing "the Popular" '. In J. Storey (ed.), *Cultural Theory and Popular Culture: A Reader*, 4th edn, London: Pearson, 508–18.

Hall, S. and Whannel, P. (2009) 'The Young Audience'. In J. Storey (ed.), *Cultural Theory and Popular Culture: A Reader*, 4th edn, London: Pearson, 45–51.

Harvey, D. (1990) *The Condition of Postmodernity*, London: Blackwell.

Hebdige, D. (1979) *Subculture: The Meaning of Style*, London: Routledge.

Hermes, J. (1995) *Reading Women's Magazines*. Cambridge: Polity Press.

Hobson, D. (1982) *Crossroads: The Drama of a Soap Opera*, London: Methuen.

Hobson, D. (1990) 'Women Audiences and the Workplace'. In M. E. Brown (ed.), *Television and Women's Culture: The Politics of the Popular*, London: Sage.

Hoggart, R. (1990) *The Uses of Literacy*, Harmondsworth: Penguin.

Iser, W. (1974) *The Implied Reader*, Baltimore, MD: Johns Hopkins University Press.

Iser, W. (1978) *The Act of Reading: A Theory of Aesthetic Response*, London: Routledge & Kegan Paul.

Jauss, H. R. (1982) *Toward an Aesthetic of Reception*, Brighton: Harvester.

Jancovich, M. (1992) 'David Morley, The Nationwide Studies'. In M. Barker and A. Beezer (eds), *Reading into Cultural Studies*, London: Routledge, 134–47.

Jenkins, H. (1992) *Textual Poachers*, New York: Routledge.

Kubey, R. and Csikszentmihalyi, M. (1990) *Television and the Quality of Life*, Hillsdale, NJ: Lawrence Erlbaum Associates.

Lacan, J. (1977) *Ecrits: A Selection*, London: Tavistock.

Laclau, E. and Mouffe, C. (1985) *Hegemony and Socialist Strategy*, London: Verso.

Laclau, E. and Mouffe, C. (2009) 'Post-Marxism without Apologies'. In J. Storey (ed.), *Cultural Theory and Popular Culture: A Reader*, 4th edn, London: Pearson, 12–19.

Laermans, R. (1993) 'Learning to Consume: Early Department Stores and the Shaping of the Modern Consumer Culture (1860–1914),' *Theory, Culture & Society* 10, 79–102.

Leavis, F. R. (1998) 'Mass Civilisation and Minority Culture'. In J. Storey (ed.), *Cultural Theory and Popular Culture*, 2nd edn, Hemel Hempstead: Prentice Hall, 13–21.

Leavis, F. R. and Thompson, D. (1977) *Culture and Environment*, Westport, CT: Greenwood Press.

Leavis, Q.D. (1978) *Fiction and the Reading Public*, London: Chatto & Windus.

Levi-Strauss, C. (1968) *Structural Anthropology*, New York: Basic Books.

Lewis, J. (1983) 'The Encoding/Decoding Model: Criticism and Redevelopments for Research on Decoding', *Media, Culture and Society* 5: 12–23.

Liebes, T. and Katz, E. (1993) *The Export of Meaning: Cross-cultural readings of Dallas*, 2nd edn, Cambridge: Polity Press.

Light, A. (1984) 'Returning to Manderley: Romance Fiction, Female Sexuality and Class', *Feminist Review* 16: 7–25.

Longhurst, D. (ed.) (1989) *Gender, Genre and Narrative Pleasure*, London: Unwin Hyman.

Lovell, T. (2009) 'Cultural Production'. In J. Storey (ed.), *Cultural Theory and Popular Culture: A Reader*, 4th edn, London: Pearson, 539–44.

Macherey, P. (1978) *A Theory of Literary Production*, London: Routledge & Kegan Paul.

McCabe, C. (1974) 'Realism and the Cinema: Notes on some Brechtian Theses', *Screen*, 15: 2, 216–35.

McLuhan, M. (1962) *The Gutenberg Galaxy*, Toronto: Toronto University Press.

McLuhan, M. (1968) *Understanding Media*, London: Sphere.

McLuhan, M. and Fiore, Q. (1967) *The Medium is the Message*, New York: Bantam and Random House.

McRobbie, A. (1991) *Feminism and Youth Culture*, London: Macmillan.

McRobbie, A. (1994) *Postmodernism and Popular Culture*, London: Routledge.

McRobbie, A. and Garber, J. (1976) 'Girls and Subcultures'. In S. Hall and T. Jefferson (eds), *Resistance through Rituals*, London: Hutchinson, 209–29.

Massey, D. (1994) *Space, Place, Gender*, Cambridge: Polity.

Marx, K. (1977) *The Eighteenth Brumaire of Louis Bonaparte*, Moscow: Progress Publishers.

Middleton, R. (1990) *Studying Popular Music*, Milton Keynes: Open University Press.

Miller, D. (1987) *Material Culture and Mass Consumption*, Oxford: Blackwell.

Miller, M. B. (1981) *The Bon Marché: Bourgeois Culture and the Department Store, 1869–1920*, Princeton, NJ: Princeton University Press.

Modleski, T. (1982) *Loving with a Vengeance: Mass-produced Fantasies for Women*, North Haven, CT: Archon Books.

Moores, S. (1993) *Interpreting Audiences*, London: Sage.

Morley, D. (1980) *The 'Nationwide' Audience*, London: British Film Institute.

Morley, D. (1986) *Family Television*, London: Comedia.

Morley, D. (1992) *Television, Audiences and Cultural Studies*, London: Routledge.

Morley, D. (1996) 'Euram, Modernity, Reason and Alterity: or Post Modernism, the Highest Stage of Cultural Imperialism'. In D. Morley and K.-H. Chen (eds), *Stuart Hall: Critical Dialogues in Cultural Studies,* London: Routledge, 326–60.

Morley, D. and Chen, K.-H. (eds) (1995) *Stuart Hall: Critical Dialogues in Cultural Studies*, London: Routledge.

References

Morris, M. (1988) 'Things to Do with Shopping Centres', in S. Sheridan (ed.), *Grafts: Feminist Cultural Criticism*, London: Verso.

Mulvey, L. (1975) 'Visual Pleasure and Narrative Cinema', *Screen* 16: 3, 6–18.

Nederveen Pieterse, J. (1995) 'Globalisation as Hybridisation', *International Sociology* 9: 2, 161–84.

Parkin, F. (1971) *Class Inequality and Political Order*, London: Paladin.

Pécheux, M. (1982) *Language, Semantics and Ideology*, London: Macmillan.

Presdee, M. (1986) 'Agony or Ecstasy: Broken Transitions and the New Social State of Working-class Youth in Australia', Occasional Papers, Magill, South Australia: South Australia Centre for Youth Studies, South Australia College of Adult Education, 21–39.

Radway, J. (1987) *Reading the Romance*, London: Verso.

Radway, J. (1988) 'Reception Study: Ethnography and the Problems of Dispersed Audiences and Nomadic Subjects', *Cultural Studies* 2: 3, 359–67.

Radway, J. (1994) 'Romance and the Work of Fantasy'. In J. Cruz and J. Lewis (eds), *Viewing, Reading, Listening: Audiences and Cultural Reception*, Boulder, CO: Westview Press, 213–31.

Ritzer, G. (1999) *The McDonaldization Thesis*, London: Sage.

Robertson, R. (1995) 'Globalization: Time-Space and Homogeneity-Heterogeneity'. In M. Featherstone, S. Lash and R. Robertson (eds), *Global Modernities*, London: Sage, 25–44.

Rojek, C. (2001) *Celebrity*, London: Reaktion.

Rosselson, L. (1979) 'Pop Music: Mobilizer or Opiate'. In C. Gardner (ed.), *Media, Politics, Culture*, London: Macmillan, 40–50.

Said, Edward (1993) *Culture and Imperialism*, New York: Vintage Books.

Saussure, F. de (1974) *Course in General Linguistics*, London: Fontana.

Schudson, M. (1984) *Advertising: The Uneasy Persuasion*, New York: Basic Books.

Schiller, H. (1979) 'Transnational Media and National Development'. In K. Nordenstreng and H. Schiller (eds), *National Sovereignty and International Communication*, Norwood, NJ: Ablex, 21–32.

Silverstone, R. (1994) *Television and Everyday Life*, London: Routledge.

Sinclair, J. (1987) *Images Incorporated*, London: Croom Helm.

Sparks, C. (1992) 'Popular Journalism: Theories and Practice'. In P. Dahlgren and C. Sparks (eds), *Journalism and Popular Culture*, London: Sage, 24–44.

Sreberny-Mohammadi, A. (1991) 'The Global and the Local in International Communications'. In J. Curran and M. Gurevitch (eds), *Mass Media and Society*, London: Arnold, 118–38

Stacey, J. (1994) *Star Gazing: Hollywood and Female Spectatorship*, London: Routledge.

Storey, J. (1992) 'Texts, Readers, Reading Formations: "My Poll and My Partner Joe" in Manchester in 1841', *Literature and History* 1: 2, 1–18.

185

Storey, J. (ed.) (1996) *What is Cultural Studies?: A Reader*, London: Edward Arnold.
Storey, J. (1999) *Cultural Consumption and Everyday Life*, London: Edward Arnold.
Storey, J. (2003) *Inventing Popular Culture*, Malden, MA: Blackwell.
Storey, J. (2009a) *Cultural Theory and Popular Culture*, Harlow: Pearson.
Storey, J. (ed.) (2009b) *Cultural Theory and Popular Culture: A Reader*, 4th edn, London: Pearson.
Storey, J. (2010) *Culture and Power in Cultural Studies*, Edinburgh: Edinburgh University Press.
Storey, J. and Johnson, D. (1994) 'The Politics of Pop and the War in the Gulf'. In J. Walsh (ed.), *The Gulf War did not Happen*, Aldershot: Arena, 101–18.
Street, J. (1986) *Rebel Rock: The Politics of Popular Music*, Oxford: Oxford University Press.
Taylor, L. (1995) 'From Psychoanalytic Feminism to Popular Feminism'. In J. Hollows and M. Jancovich (eds), *Approaches to Popular Film*, Manchester: Manchester University Press, 151–71.
Tomlinson, J. (1997) 'Internationalism, Globalization and Cultural Imperialism'. In K. Thompson (ed.), *Media and Regulation*, London: Sage, 117–62.
Tomlinson, J. (1999) *Globalization and Culture*, Cambridge: Polity Press.
Tunstall, J. (1978) *The Media are American*, London: Constable.
Turner, G. (2003) *British Cultural Studies*, 3rd edn, London: Routledge.
Turner, G. (2004) *Understanding Celebrity*, London: Sage.
Turner, G. (2009) *The Demotic Turn*, London: Sage.
Vickery, A. (1993) 'Women and the World of Goods: A Lancashire Consumer and her Possessions, 1751–81'. In J. Brewer and R. Porter (eds), *Consumption and the World of Goods*, London: Routledge, 274–301.
Volosinov, V. (1973) *Marxism and the Philosophy of Language*, London: Seminar Press.
Williams, R. H. (1982) *Dream Worlds: Mass Consumption in Late Nineteenth-Century France*, Berkeley CA: University of California Press.
Williams, R. (1990) *Television, Technology and Cultural Form*, 2nd edn, London: Routledge.
Willis, P. (1978) *Profane Culture*, London: Routledge & Kegan Paul.
Winship, J. (1987) *Inside Women's Magazines*, London: Pandora.
Wright, W. (1975) *Sixguns and Society*, Berkeley, CA: University of California Press.

INDEX

187